Day by Day

DAY BY DAY

MEDITATIONS ON
RICHARD OF CHICHESTER'S PRAYER

FREDERICK BORSCH

SPCK

Originally published in the United States of America in 2009
as *Day by Day: Loving God More Dearly*
by Morehouse Publishing

First published in Great Britain in 2009 as
Day by Day: Meditations on Richard of Chichester's Prayer by

Society for Promoting Christian Knowledge
36 Causton Street
London SW1P 4ST

by permission of Morehouse Publishing,
an imprint of Church Publishing Incorporated,
445 Fifth Avenue, New York, NY 10016

British Library Cataloguing-in-Publication Data
A catalogue record for this book is available from the British Library

ISBN 978–0–281–06142–6

1   3   5   7   9   10   8   6   4   2

Typeset by Vicki Black
Printed in Great Britain by Ashford Colour Press

Produced on paper from sustainable forests

To students, faculty, staff, and friends of the
Berkeley Divinity School at Yale, Yale Divinity School,
and the Lutheran Theological Seminary at Philadelphia

CONTENTS

one

RICHARD'S PRAYER

Day by day, dear Lord, of you three things I pray:
to see you more clearly,
love you more dearly,
follow you more nearly,
day by day.

This prayer seems so familiar. It may be best known from the musical *Godspell*, with its hip Jesus and his shrewd parables, while its petitions have also been set to music in a number of hymns and anthems.[1] Many of us have prayed with thoughts and words like these, if not in these very phrases. In many ways profound, it is, as we shall see, also so simple a hymn—a plea of trust and need, so yearning and hopeful.

Christian tradition traces the heart of the prayer to the thirteenth-century bishop and saint known as Richard of

Chichester.[2] Its earliest source is the story of Richard's life
by his companion and confessor, Ralph Bocking. Richard
is said to have prayed as he lay dying,

> Thanks be to you, my Lord Jesus Christ, for all the
> benefits which you have given me, for all the pains
> and insults you have borne for me, O most merciful
> Redeemer, Friend, and Brother. May I know you
> more clearly, love you more dearly, and follow you
> more nearly.

We may well believe that Richard's friends and companions remembered and then continued to use his threefold
petitions to see, to love, and to follow the Lord in their own
prayers. The phrase "day by day" may have been added later;
perhaps whoever did so believed they heard the thought in
the melody of the prayer. Or possibly, in one way or
another, "day by day, dear Lord, three things I pray" also
goes back to a time in Richard's life. Whatever its precise
origins, the words of this prayer have been on the lips of
many Christians in subsequent generations as they prayed
in longing, love, and service.

We can imagine Bishop Richard whispering the prayer
in his last days, but we may also suppose that he would have
offered these or similar petitions throughout the life in
which he grew to sainthood. Richard was remembered for
his humility, his perseverance in times of hardship, and the
strength and generosity of his faith. He also inspired many
because of his care for the poor, widows, and orphans, and
those who were sick. After his death in 1253, miracles of
healing were said to have taken place through his interces-
sion and a shrine grew up at his cathedral in Chichester, a
small city south of London and a few miles from the
English Channel. His had been a life of close friendships

and high position, but also of opposition, exile, and poverty.
Certainly there must have been many days of challenge and
of life's ills and vagaries. The intonations of a brave and
searching man on his knees can be heard throughout this
prayer.

Richard's earliest biographer, the Dominican friar who
had been his companion and confessor, knew this man of
prayer well. There were occasions, Friar Ralph Bocking tells
us, when early visitors to his chapel would find the bishop
already there, having spent the night in prayer. On other
days he would rise "before the birds were awake" and, while
his chaplains still slept, be at his prayers before the day's
work was begun.

Richard was also known as a man of discipline and
order, a man of laws who could be fierce in his sense of
justice and fairness toward others. Through much of his life
he was esteemed as a careful administrator and a strict disciplinarian. As bishop he drew up statutes by which he
expected clergy and laity to live. While strong in his support
and defense of his clergy, those who were lazy or living
immorally earned his rebuke. He was a reformer. He
expected that the parish clergy would be well instructed
and about their business as teachers and pastors. They were
to dress cleanly. Vestments and the fabric of churches should
be in good condition. Church buildings should be kept in
repair and uncluttered. The prayers and offices were to be
said "roundly"; that is, audibly and distinctly, without
hurried or garbled words. Given the problems and challenges in the church and society, such discipline and moral
leadership were no doubt needed. Richard wanted right
living, diligence, honesty, and prayerfulness for the sake of all
the people in the care of the diocese.

And yet his biographer maintained that Richard was remembered first and foremost as "jolly, warm-hearted, courteous, and of a cheerful countenance." His very name, Friar Ralph inventively suggests, was made up from the parts of three words, *RIdens, CARus,* and *DUlciS:* "laughing, beloved, and gracious." This combination in one person of a reformer and organized defender of laws with one who is yet often jolly, courteous, and gracious is unusual at the very least. The respect and affection in which this man of grace and spirit was held evidently was the fruit of his own example—the discipline began with him. A bishop, he believed, should be of irreproachable life, sober, restrained, and hospitable. He was "addicted," it is said, to works of mercy. When visiting a parish, Richard would inquire about those who were sick or poor and go to them with money and words of comfort. When they died, he would, whenever he was able, help bury them with his own hands. He evidently had the capacity, as Paul put it, to "rejoice with those who rejoice" and to "weep with those who weep" (Romans 12:15).

Temperate at table, the bishop preferred meals of bread dipped in beer or wine even in times of festival. He had practiced forms of asceticism at various times in his life, and his dress, too, was modest, usually a tunic covered with a linen cape. In winter he added a wool mantle that, in time, became rather threadbare. He lived simply so that he would not be set too far apart from those of low estate in his pastoral care. In an age when some bishops lived, as the saying goes, "high off the hog" and were often absent from their dioceses, following the king about and tending to matters of state, Richard hardly ever left his diocese. Because he had experienced exile and homelessness at one time in his life, and knew what it was like to be poor and outcast, he loved to give things away—which was seldom to the liking of his stewards and bailiffs, who were more concerned about restoring the fortunes of the diocese.

People who are regarded as saints in their lifetime can be thought to be somewhat otherworldly and probably not much good at the practical details of life. Yet Richard was skilled, energetic, and attentive to the arts of administration. This jolly man, who often went about with a cheerful smile on his face, had a will that seemed conformed to the service of others. People sensed in him an inner consecration of life.

How did he become this way? We can picture him often offering up the heartfelt petitions of his "dear Lord, three things I pray." We can hear him repeating his prayer as a young student and then teacher at Oxford; as Chancellor of the University and later for the Archbishop of Canterbury; after that in exile, trying to find his way to love and follow his Lord; as Bishop of Chichester; and then finally, as he lay dying. One sees him kneeling in chapel and churches, in his study, walking about his diocese, wanting to show God's love for others, keeping faithfully to his ministry of administration, visiting the poor. Not only did this prayer inform and shape his life, it grew from his life as well—from his times of hardships and uncertainty, out of his hopes and deepest aspirations. These times of earnest prayer would have formed the words of his mind and heart: "to see you more clearly, love you more dearly, follow you more nearly, dear Lord." In these ways the prayer becomes the story of his life. The prayer offers us the lineaments of his biography—the life story of a man determined yet kind, questing and firm in his faith to know, love, and follow his Lord.

Informed by Prayer

Desmond Tutu of South Africa is another bishop of great compassion and a strong sense of justice. Many of us would call him a saint, whose capacity for courage and graciousness, for determination and joy easily reminds us of Richard of Chichester. Desmond tells me that he has used Richard's prayer to see, love, and follow "for donkey's years" (as he puts it in his inimitable fashion). He believes his life, too, has been informed by the prayer, for Desmond Tutu also has experienced times of harsh opposition and persecution as well as high office and heavy administrative responsibilities. He was fierce in his struggles against the evils of apartheid and in his calls for justice and regard for the dignity of each human being. Yet all who have known him also picture his often smiling face and can hear his laughter.

That mirthfulness flows from his trust in the love of God in the very midst of some of the world's greatest suffering and wrongs. It may well have been Desmond's greatest strength and weapon against apartheid, for, he would frequently let people know, in God's eyes apartheid and all forms of discrimination were silly. "God," I can hear him insisting even now, "loves each and every one of you."

> Now just tell me, what does the color of a person's skin tell you about that person? Does the color of a person's skin tell you whether the person is intelligent? Does it tell you if that person is loving? Supposing we said that the thing that determines

privilege is the size of your nose? Now, I have a large nose—supposing we said that people with large noses are the privileged people? And they say now, "Ah, you want to go to a toilet; that toilet is reserved only for large noses." If you have a small nose you are going to be in trouble. That university, you enter only if you have a large nose like mine. If you have a small nose, then you must apply to the Ministry of Small Nose Affairs for permission to attend the university for large noses.[3]

It takes a strong and deep faith to be able to make fun of human folly and wickedness, to be able to smile and laugh, when so many things in life are painful and unjust. It is the faith also of Julian of Norwich in the century following Richard who, in the middle of plague, illness, and many troubles, held that yet "all will be well, all will be well, all manner thing will be well." Such a response calls for much prayer, compassion, and a readiness to reach out with love and forgiveness for others—even and perhaps especially for one's enemies, who are also loved by God. It takes a heart that beats to the rhythm of a threefold prayer asking to see, to love, and to follow our Lord.

In reflecting on this prayer and the life it shaped, it is important to remember that Richard's life and times were in many ways radically different from our own. Science, technology, medicine, and the profusion of information about other times and places have given us greater knowledge and understanding but also distance us from the ways and beliefs of thirteenth-century England. We live in different cultures. Our lives and experiences are not the same. We will need to respect these differences as we reflect on Richard's life, ministries, and prayer in these meditations.

Yet, surely, we may also find similarities and parallels with our own lives—our own times of hardship and uncertainty, our searching, our hopes and deepest aspirations to see and know, to love and put into practice what matters most to us in life. We, too, want eyes that look to what we most care about—lives of both courage and gracefulness, of commitment and the smile of faith; lives formed by our own ways of praying to come ever closer to God.

We do well to remember, too, that Christians never pray alone. Even if we are on a solitary walk or in our own room, prayer is always praying together—the prayer of a people of yearning and faith, a people praying for one another and supporting one another in prayer. In a congregation but also across congregational and denominational lines, across ethnic and national and gender and class differences, across time zones and even the generations—in the communion of saints, the ancient and ongoing prayer continues. We can imagine that Richard sometimes prayed "these three things" with Ralph Bocking, with his friends Edmund and Simon, in community worship in chapel and cathedral. We can imagine that we, along with Richard of Chichester and Desmond Tutu and with sisters and brothers at home and around the world and through the years, are praying with one another the same prayer to "see you more clearly, love you more dearly, follow you more nearly, day by day."

two

TO SEE YOU
MORE CLEARLY

Amid life's changes and uncertainties we long for some
clarity of vision. In the midst of perplexities we hope
to see and to know what is to be prized above all—what is
worth life's service. Richard and many others have aspired
to see more clearly the longed-for goodness and beauty at
the heart of existence. Circumscribed by mortality, we, too,
pray to know some purpose in and for a creation. We ask
why there is a world and life at all—what could it be for?
As life goes on, buffeted by loss and tragedy, we yearn for
coherence—a *logos* or reason and center that might hold
things together, a story for life. Hearts hope for a beginning
and goal, and at least a glimpse of the One who might
sustain and inspire the human adventure.

I can imagine Richard as a young man starting to form
this hope and this prayer "to see" his Lord and God "more
clearly" in his own life. There are slightly different versions

of this first petition as it has been handed down to us—is it "to *know* you more clearly" or "to *see* you more clearly"? Richard would have frequently used Latin, and the Latin verb *scio* (from which comes our word "science") would most often have been translated "to know," which has also the meanings of "to understand" and "to perceive." One can imagine that the version "to see you more clearly" arose from this related meaning, for seeing is, of course, a way of knowing—as suggested in the adage "Seeing is believing."

We might picture him in these early years with dark hair and clear brown eyes, strong of bone and lanky, already hardened from farm labor. Richard was born near the end of the twelfth century in a town called Droitwich, in the west of England, near Worcester. For much of his life he was known as Richard of Wyche, a family name that may have been derived from the *wyches* or salt springs in the area. With his sister and an older brother to whom he remained close for most of his life, Richard lost his father, a prosperous farmer, and then his mother at an early age. Much of their inheritance was dissipated by their guardians, but even as a young man Richard showed considerable skill in helping his less diligent older brother manage the farm left to them. He plowed and pruned; he labored long and hard. But, with the farm improved, he left it to his brother.

He had determined to become a scholar, and so he set off for Oxford when he was in his mid-teens. Tales were later told of his poverty as a student. Such stories might seem the product of pious imagination, but Oxford was a poor community—one of simple inns and halls rather than the handsome colleges that would later be designed and built. It would have been common for students at the time to sleep two or more to a bed and share their coat with friends. We may hope that there were at least a few days of feasting from time to time, but bread and thin soup, eaten from a wooden board and bowl, was the regular meal.

The thirteenth century was a time of considerable ferment and new learning. Richard, who had probably begun his studies with the Benedictine monks in Worcester, would have first studied the basic *trivium* of grammar, rhetoric, and dialectic, and then the *quadrivium* of arithmetic, astronomy, music, and geometry. One of his Oxford tutors, who became a mentor and lifelong friend, was the saintly Edmund Rich, later the Archbishop of Canterbury. Robert Grosseteste, renowned scholar and later a strong and influential Bishop of Lincoln, was another of his teachers. Grosseteste translated Aristotle from the Greek and was interested in astronomy, optics, and mathematics. Along with Edmund and Robert, Richard would have felt the influence of the Fourth Lateran Council of 1215 that provided considerable energy for church reform by advocating more learning for the clergy. The Council also sought greater recognition for the authority of Pope Innocent III, which meant that tensions between the church in Rome and the English king Henry III continued, as did the tests of strength between the king and his barons and bishops, not least on matters of ecclesiastical appointments and wealth.

By 1220 Richard had become established as a twenty-three-year-old scholar and was himself beginning to be a teacher. To England and Oxford in this decade came members of the new Dominican order of friars intent on reform and seeking a more rigorous and dedicated practice of Christian learning and living. Early on, Richard was greatly attracted to their ways of devotion and service. They were soon followed by Franciscans, still struggling with their commitment to strict poverty. Although favored by

the outwardly pious English king Henry III, the friars were
not welcomed by all; problems arose with the local clergy
over questions of money and authority. But these Domini-
cans and Franciscans made rich contributions to theological discussions and debates, and, especially in this time of
reform, to ethics and questions about faithful Christian
living: how could those who dedicated themselves to the
Lord Jesus best follow and serve him in their lives and
ministries?

The more formal study of theology at Oxford would
have been postgraduate work pursued by relatively few. The
Bible would have been a major academic focus for Richard,
along with a famous collection by the scholastic Peter
Lombard called *The Four Books of Sentences,* his *magnum opus*
that became a standard textbook for all medieval universities. It was a comprehensive collection of excerpts from the
Bible, the church fathers, and later medieval scholars upon
every aspect of theology.

A third major area of study, and that which most occu-
pied Richard, was canon law—a compendium of doctrine
and governance that guided not only the church's mission
and governance but also, since there was no separation of
church and state, many aspects of social and political life.
Canon law was canon theology as well, for it derived from
a theological understanding of the world as created and ultimately ruled over by God. It provided a vision of a regulated secular order that reflected the moral ordering of life
by the divine. A man of the time who was educated in
canon law would be at once a theologian, an ethicist, and a
lawyer.

In order to pursue his studies of canon law Richard trav-
eled to Paris, another university center of the international
church. Later, it would seem, he studied in Bologna as well.

He would have spent many hours reading and discussing a voluminous compendium of laws called the *Decretum,* which was compiled in Bologna a century earlier by a monk and jurist known as Gratian. This legal textbook was an effort to systematize a vast amount of canon law and commentary going back over a thousand years.

In addition to regulating every detail of daily life in medieval society, an important concern of canon law was justice for every child of God—and not least justice for the poor in society. Based on what we know of his later conduct, young Richard would seem to have been especially attracted to this legal guidance. Following scriptural teaching regarding care for the widows, orphans, the poor, and strangers, canon law guaranteed certain rights for those of low status. Relief of poverty was a matter of justice as well as charity, and the laws called for an equitable distribution of wealth in which the rights of private property were not absolute, but qualified by some sense of community property. Anyone rightly interpreting canon law had to be concerned with maintenance of the legal rights of the poor in society and with the administration of the institutions that provided poor relief. No doubt Richard found in these teachings not only inspiration but challenge for his life of service.

One imagines the young Richard, now in his late twenties, well-schooled and up-and-coming in the world of church and state. It is reported that he more than once turned down the opportunity for an advantageous marriage so that he could more ardently pursue what he felt to be his vocation. He wanted to be able to understand and interpret the teaching and laws of the church as they were intended to describe God's ways for society. It is not hard to think of him praying these words from Psalm 119.

How can a young man keep his way pure?
  By guarding it according to your word.
With my whole heart I seek you;
  do not let me stray from your commandments.
I treasure your word in my heart,
  so that I many not sin against you.
Blessed are you, O LORD;
  teach me your statutes.
With my lips I declare
  all the ordinances of your mouth.
I delight in the ways of your decrees
  as much as in all riches.
I will mediate on your precepts,
  and fix my eyes on your ways.
I will delight in your statutes;
  I will not forget your word. (Psalm 119:9–16)

Perhaps it was during these years that Richard prayed so ardently to see his Lord and to know God's purposes more clearly.

God Unseen While Overheard

Yet no one has ever had a clear vision or knowledge of the Lord of all life. "No one has ever seen God." Richard would have known well this truth set forth in the opening chapter of the Gospel of John (1:18) and maintained through much of scripture. He would have heard Job longing to meet and contest with the God "who alone stretched out the heavens," the One "who made the Bear and Orion, the Pleiades." Signs of this Creator "who does great things beyond understanding, and marvelous things without number" may be seen everywhere. But Job complains, "Look, he passes by me, and I do not see him; he moves on, but I do not perceive him" (Job 9:8–11).

God's presence can be symbolized in various ways. Figures of speech and images invite the imagining of God's nearness. In one dramatic instance God is wondrously and mysteriously present to Moses in a transfigured bush. The bush burns without burning up. It is ever-living while ever-giving in its flames of light and life. Yet, striking as the image is, this is still only a sign. The essence of the divine life, the source of all creation, remains beyond the world of human seeing. God's presence is figuratively hinted. Holiness and inexhaustible power and life are alluded to, while the Divine continues to transcend creaturely ways of knowing—of being able to say, *Now I know that I have seen God. I have seen the beauty and grandeur of God.*

Moses, scripture tells us, comes as near as anyone to seeing God. Trying to lead the balky people of Israel through privation and temptation to the promised land, the great prophet seeks assurance of God's presence (Exodus 33). God promises to send an angel into the land ahead of the people. There is a pillar of fire by night and of cloud by day that both signals and hides the divine holiness. Were, however, the people to come directly into contact with this holiness, it would consume them. Moses is said to speak to God "face to face, as one speaks to a friend," but any suggestion that Moses had actually seen God's face is quickly corrected. "No one shall see me and live." Instead Moses is allowed to stand in a cleft of a rock, his eyes covered by the hand of God until God has passed by. "Then I will take

away my hand, you shall see my back; but my face shall not
be seen." The story, which has led to ribald jokes about God
showing Moses only his backside, nicely makes its point
regarding the mystery of God's presence. Sometimes it may
only be afterward, looking back, as it were, in the remembering and retelling, that one may realize the presence of
God has been intimated.

More often in scripture it seems by some manner of
hearing rather than sight that God's presence can be realized. Still, however, there is a note of mystery. In that story
of the burning bush that Richard would often have
pondered, Moses sees that "the bush was blazing, yet it was
not consumed" (Exodus 3:2). He then hears a voice calling
him by name and telling him that the God of his ancestors
is wonderfully here: "I am the God of your father, the God
of Abraham, the God of Isaac, and the God of Jacob." In
response, Moses hides his face, "for he was afraid to look at
God" (3:6). It is not hard to imagine ourselves in Moses'
shoes, or rather standing on that holy ground barefooted,
amazed, and frightened, having removed our shoes at God's
command. There we, too, could well bow low and bury our
eyes in our hands.

God next tells Moses of his purpose to rescue the
chosen people from oppression in Egypt and to bring them
to "a good and broad land, a land flowing with milk and
honey" (3:8). But, if he is to be God's agent in this, Moses
wants more identification, as it were, more identity from
this God. The people are going to ask him for this; they will
want to know more about this God with such an extraordinary agenda. What is Moses to say when they ask, "What
is his name?" Having a name would not only bring more
identity and definition to this God of the ancestors, but it
might also give the people some claim on God's attention.

But to this request the voice responds in notoriously ambiguous syllables, often translated as "I am who I am" or, perhaps better, "I will be who I will be" (3:14). It is a name and yet not a name. God's presence can be *heard,* but God's very being is ultimately elusive; it cannot be seen by the eye or fully comprehended by human hearing or knowing.

In other biblical stories the sound of God's presence can also be surprising, even bewildering, concealing as well as revealing. To Job it comes fearsomely "out of the whirlwind," telling him how little he knows of God and God's ways (Job 38–39). By way of contrast, the prophet Elijah finds the Lord God not in a great wind, earthquake, or fire, but in "a sound of sheer silence" (1 Kings 19:11–12). Other prophets tell of God's *words* to them: the "word of the Lord" comes to Jeremiah, Isaiah, Ezekiel, Amos, Hosea, and others. Yet even with respect to such hearing, there is usually something enigmatic—a measure of uncertainty, together with an awareness that words are, as it were, *slippery*; their meaning is impossible fully to pin down. Sometimes the uncertainty is represented by what may seem like a contradiction when two different stories about God's will are laid side by side. In one version of Israel's history the anointing of Saul as king and the establishment of his monarchy is a sign of divine favor; in another version we hear that the demands of the people to have a king ruling over them have displeased God and will lead to considerable misery (1 Samuel 8–10). Those seeking to comprehend the Lord's dealings with God's people are told by the prophet Isaiah, "My thoughts are not your thoughts, nor are your ways my ways, says the LORD" (Isaiah 55:8). It is as though we cannot fully or definitively *know* God through direct speech; the divine thoughts and ways are different from ours. Revelation

comes, but questions of interpretation will always compli-
cate efforts fully to comprehend.

"I am God and no mortal," God reminds the prophet
Hosea (11:9). God may be spoken of in human terms, but
any human analogies for God's activity can only be figura-
tive and approximate. In one rendition of Paul's conversion
experience in the Acts of the Apostles, for example, the
people standing by hear a voice but see no one (Acts 9:7).
In another version they see a light but hear no voice (Acts
22:9). In the Gospel of John, when Jesus hears a voice from
heaven, some of the bystanders said that it was thunder,
while others thought it was the voice of angel (John 12:29).

Rabbis of Jesus' time sometimes spoke of "the daughter
of the voice" or a kind of echo of God's words. It is as when
we hear an echo. We are sure that we have heard a sound.
We may even feel certain that we have been called. But
where exactly did it come from and how is it to be understood? These are various ways of indicating that there is
always a mysterious and at times even puzzling dimension
to the *voice* of God. God is, as it were, *overheard*. There may
be moments when the nearness of the Holy One seems
overwhelming and undeniable, while yet the God who is
close by and present to our experience is also transcendent
and beyond all human sensibility.

The Soul Longs for You

The differing stories about how Israel obtained a king (as a sign of God's purpose or because of Israel's willful demands) also illustrate a tension between divine providence and human freedom found in the Bible. Is God directing what happens, or is God letting events take their own course? Is God taking care of Israel, or is God a long way off, even abandoning the people to their own devices? Or, in the mysterious ways of God's providence, can God act alongside or through human freedom, and even through the turning away from God and sin?

Richard would many times have heard the saga of the willful King David, who is yet chosen of God (1 Samuel 16 through 1 Kings 2). God sees to David's anointing and does not forget the promise to him that "there shall never fail you a successor before me to sit on the throne of Israel" (1 Kings 8:25). God can be heard staying by David through thick and thin, both to bless and to judge severely when David goes his own ways, such as his sin with Bathsheba and, most particularly, his betrayal of his loyal soldier Uriah. David's life is a kind of microcosm for the whole story of the people of God, trying to follow God, but then losing and yet again finding their Lord through exodus, the promised land, exile, and return. Then there is the still larger biblical drama of human freedom and divine providence that begins in the loss of innocence in creation's garden and passes through Gethsemane's fear and passion to the hope and wonder of the third garden of paradise.

Yet in all this drama a measure of longing, uncertainty, and even fear seems inescapable. How can people be sure of God's presence and favor? The Hebrew scriptures call forth a faith and trust in God, whose presence and ways cannot be clearly known, even as the people Israel continually yearn for this God.

> As a deer long for flowing streams,
>   so my soul longs for you, O God.
> My soul thirsts for God,
>   for the living God.
> When shall I come and behold
>   the face of God? (Psalm 42:1–2)

One can imagine young Richard, along with disciples like ourselves before and after, singing and praying the opening words of Psalm 63: "O, God, you are my God; eagerly I seek you." We long as with a parched thirsting: "My soul thirsts for you, my flesh faints for you, as in a barren and dry land where there is no water." The soul seeks a sanctuary where, by the graciousness of God who is beyond all knowing, God's presence might still be granted.

> Therefore I have gazed upon you
>   in your holy place,
>   that I might behold your power and your glory.
> For your loving-kindness is better than life itself;
>   my lips shall give you praise.
> So will I bless you as long as I live
>   and lift up my hands in your Name.
>   (Psalm 63:2–4, BCP)

An often repeated figure of speech in the Psalms is the prayer that God's *face* might be seen. A number of the Psalms pray that the Lord will show the light of the divine countenance and that God's face will shine upon the people (see 4:6, 31:16). The imagery suggests a scene in which individuals are entering the royal court hoping that the monarch will lift the royal countenance and smile radiantly with favor. "Let your face shine, that we may be saved" (Psalm 80:3). By way of fearful contrast, Job asks, "Why do you hide your face, and count me as your enemy?" (Job 13:24), and the psalmist cries out, "O LORD, why do you cast me off? Why do you hide your face from me?" (Psalm 88:14). The biblical narrative is this story of repeatedly finding but then losing God's favor—while always there is renewed hope and prayer, since "for God alone my soul waits in silence" (Psalm 62:1).

The waiting can sometimes be agonizing. Where is this so keenly intuited yet hidden presence?

> Why, O LORD, do you stand far off?
> Why do you hide yourself in times of trouble?
> (Psalm 10:1)

This absence can seem as though God has gone to sleep:

> Rouse yourself! Why do you sleep, O Lord?
> Awake, do not cast us off forever!
> Why do you hide your face?
> Why do you forget our affliction and oppression?
> (Psalm 44:23–24)

The psalmist's words, full of the fear of abandonment, are wrenched out again in Jesus' cry from the cross that echoes so poignantly through the annals of human suffering: "My God, my God, why have you forsaken me?" (Psalm 22:1; Mark 15:34).

Overwhelming Awe

Richard of Chichester would have known and prayed all these scripture verses of hope and longing. He would also have experienced the hiddenness of God. There must have been times when he, like all of us, sought distraction in entertainments, in overworking, in looking for and at other things rather than looking for the heart of life. And, if the problem of not being able to see and know God was a challenge for people of biblical times, as it must have been for Richard in his own day, surely it must seem even greater for us who live in a world so far removed from that of the Bible.

We have some awareness and historical insight into how the biblical narratives were written down and collected by human beings. However much we may believe God's Spirit was speaking through the people and events narrated in the Bible, we also recognize that scripture's words were shaped in the most human and time-bound of ways. In the same way, we have an historical perspective on the conditions and worldview of a figure from eight hundred years ago, like Richard. Nowadays scientific knowledge helps us to explain events such as eclipses and earthquakes, hurricanes, plagues and tsunamis—events that were once thought to be caused directly by divine agency. We are aware in our time that all is being played out in a universe believed to have trillions upon trillions of stars in more than one hundred billion galaxies in what is conceivably one of but many universes. Our awe abounds, but it also overwhelms us. How could we even imagine that we could turn and look upon God? In what direction would we face? Where and when could God possibly be known? As the psalmist gives cry, we too continue to pray, "My soul thirsts for God, for the living God. When shall I come and behold the face of God?" (Psalm 42:2). Where is the beauty, the source, and the goal for the goodness we pray may be found at the heart of life?

Our Awareness

As we pray and wonder, we may also stop to be amazed that we are doing so. There is an *I* and a *me* here in this vast universe to have these feelings and thoughts! How is it that we have our sense of self-awareness and of the world about us?

When we pause like this we may find ourselves trying to come to some understanding of our own consciousness, to become more reflective about our thinking and our aware-ness of self and others. We do not know how our capacity not only to think, but also to think about our thinking and to reflect on our self-awareness has come about. We recog-nize that evolutionary processes have favored certain forms of consciousness, such as the ability to avoid dangers and to seek out food and to reproduce one's own kind. But human consciousness has developed in ways that seem to go beyond the benefits of evolution. Some scientists regard our awareness of self—a kind of superconsciousness—as an accidental by-product of evolution.

Whatever its cause, with human awareness of the self and others has also come a consciousness of time, and with this has come story, language, creativity, responsibility, and love. We are able to consider what is in our own self-interest and at least to imagine the self-interest of others. We are able to come to a vision of the common good. The flexibility of our brains and consciousness has allowed us to *convert* certain strategies for survival into the ability to do algebra, to make poetry and music, and to tell jokes. Beyond mere survival we can value what is comic, lovely, and joyous along with the suffering and tragedy of human life.

With this awareness there also, however, comes the capacity for self-criticism and judgment, which are part of the workings of conscience. We become aware of time passing, our aging and our mortality, our missed opportunities. Sometimes we would just as soon escape our heightened sense of awareness, and perhaps we do so in the benign blessing of sleep. At other times we try to dull our self-awareness with various entertainments and distractions or, more disturbingly, with alcohol, drugs, sexual or other addictions, or seeking riches or forms of speed and dangerous living. We can get the blues or become depressed and even imagine the ultimate escape of death. Perhaps there are days when we wish we were less attuned to the universe and the world around us, although then we would not be fully human and experience all of life's color and pageantry, its heartbreaks and opportunities for sharing life and love with others.

Spirit and Spirit

While such questioning, wonder, and longing are vital parts of the human story, Richard would also have experienced, as is true for many of us, times when human awareness seems, perhaps surprisingly, not alone. God remains unseen, and words to describe the slaking of the longing thirst for God are hard to come by, but our awareness can be startled to discover that it is not without company.

Richard of Wyche would have known of another Richard who was born in Britain a quarter of a century earlier. Richard of St. Victor, who came to be prior of the famous Augustinian abbey of St. Victor in Paris, was a theologian and mystic who once advised in his treatise *The Mystical Ark,* "If you wish to search out the deep things of God, search out first of all the depths of your own spirit."[4] Richard of St. Victor was one of many men and women of prayer who have counseled that there is some link, some compatibility of relationship, between our human aware-ness and the Spirit of God. In the next century the author of *The Cloud of Unknowing* wrote, "Strain every nerve in every possible way to know and experience yourself as you truly are. It will not be long, I suspect, before you have a real knowledge and experience of God as God is."[5] In this way human awareness, or what we could also call human spirit or soul, becomes a clue to the divine awareness—God's Spirit. Humanity is said to be created in the image of God: "Then God said, 'Let us make humankind in our image, according to our likeness'" (Genesis 1:26). God, of course, is not human, but if we humans are in some way created in God's likeness, then the divine graciousness may allow us to imagine God in some way to be related to our image. All figures of speech are inadequate, but God's desire for us, one may believe, enables the Spirit God to inhabit the imagining of our awareness in its longing to know God.

In this intimate relationship of human and divine awareness—of spirit and Spirit—there would have to be times when it is difficult to be clear about the relationship—even where we end, as it were, and God begins. Augustine was among those who have prayed to the God who is nearer than his inmost being, what he called in his *Confessions* the "life of my soul." It is in this intimacy, he believed, that we begin to understand who we truly are. In prayer there is frequently the experience more of being known than knowing—of being seen rather than seeing. To see would be in some sense to comprehend God. Instead, one is comprehended. "Now I know only in part," intuited Paul; "then I will know fully, even as I have been fully known" (1 Corinthians 13:12). In like manner the psalmist meditates:

> O LORD, you have searched me
>   and known me.
> You know when I sit down and when I rise up;
>   you discern my thoughts from far away.
> You search out my path and my lying down,
>   and are acquainted with all my ways.
> Even before a word is on my tongue,
>   O LORD, you know it completely.
> You hem me in, behind and before,
>   and lay your hand upon me.

Such knowledge is too wonderful for me;
  it is so high that I cannot attain it.
Where can I go from your spirit?
  Or where can I flee from your presence?
                              (Psalm 139:1–7)

"As God knows me," John Donne wrote in a sermon, "so shall I know God, but I shall not know God as God knows me."[6] This hidden God, one comes to believe, is mysteriously and awesomely aware of us. We are present, not to another being that we can point to or prove, but to that which might be imagined as the Awareness of all being—that which "lets be" all in existence. In God, Paul tells the Athenians, quoting an ancient way of apprehending divine Presence, "we live and move and have our being" (Acts 17:28). This is God, whose circumference is nowhere and whose center is everywhere. In the words of an old Irish hymn he would have known, Richard may well have prayed:

Be thou my vision, O Lord of my heart;
all else be nought to me, save that thou art—
thou my best thought, by day or by night,
waking or sleeping, thy presence my light.

Be thou my wisdom, and thou my true word;
I ever with thee and thou with me, Lord;
thou my great Father; thine own may I be;
thou in my dwelling, and I one with thee.

High King of heaven, when victory is won,
may I reach heaven's joys, bright heaven's Sun!
Heart of my heart, whatever befall,
still be my vision, O Ruler of all. (Hymn 488)[7]

In the Image of God

The vision to which this hymn attests is, however, no human possession. We are far more comprehended than comprehending. However much we may sense being in God's presence, there remains much about the character and intentionality of the divine awareness that is unknown to us. But, then, at the heart of Richard's faith and prayer was his belief that God has done something amazing. While in so many ways beyond comprehending, God has made a yet more special use of the image of God. Through Jesus, God has lived into the *imago Dei*—as the link between transcendent and human life. Richard believed that in Jesus we have been given the chief clue to understanding God's very character and hopes for humanity. In human life and flesh we have been given Jesus as Lord and Savior and Friend.

Jesus, we hear through the words of scripture, proclaimed the coming of the kingdom of God. The reign of God he proclaimed was not a place, but a way—God's way, which could already begin to come "on earth as it is in heaven" (Matthew 6:10). In the reign of God the poor are blessed, along with the merciful and the peacemakers. Blessed, too, are the pure in heart, and those who hunger and thirst for what is right and fair in life. All are invited to live by these ways. Everyone can be accepted, forgiven, and included.

And Jesus not only spoke of God's ways: he also lived them out in his life and ministry. As his disciples came to see, they could learn the ways of God from the ways of

Jesus. He not only *told* parables of the kingdom; by *enacting* them he became God's parable in human life and story. He not only talked of inviting everyone into the kingdom, he did so—by reaching out to the wounded and poor, to the sin-sick and lame, to Bartimaeus, Zacchaeus, and Legion, to the Samaritan woman by the well and the Canaanite woman whose daughter needed healing. Jesus had not only spoken the words of God; he was now in person the Word of God.

And the Spirit of God that seemed to indwell his life became known as *his* Spirit. He did not leave his followers comfortless after the self-offering of his death. As the disciples came to believe in his new life, they found the Spirit of God to be like Jesus. In this Spirit of Jesus they remembered and told his stories again. They broke the bread and shared the wine. *This is my body, given for you. . . . This is my blood, poured out for you.* This Spirit, coming "in my name, will teach you everything, and remind you of all that I have said to you" (John 14:26).

"No one has ever seen God," the evangelist reminds us. "It is God the only Son, who is close to the Father's heart, who has made him known" (John 1:18). When Richard prayed to see and know God more clearly, it was this clue in human life—the Word, this parable of God's Spirit—that was foremost in his heart and mind. This was the one to whom he prayed as "Redeemer, Friend, and Brother."

Often Richard would have heard the Fourth Evangelist's meditation on this faith in Jesus. The disciple Philip asks for what all of us long for: "Lord, show us the Father." "Have I been with you all this time," Jesus responds, "and you still do not know me? Whoever has seen me has seen the Father. . . . Believe me that I am in the Father and the Father is in me" (John 14:8–9, 11). "Whoever sees me sees him

who sent me" (John 12:45); "The Father and I are one"
(John 10:30). This Son, in the analogies of the Letter to the
Hebrews, is "the reflection of God's glory": God is no
mortal, yet in this mortal we see "the exact imprint of God's
very being" (Hebrews 1:3).

The mystical mutuality of the will and love of God and
Jesus is given further theological expression when Paul
makes explicit the faith that Christ Jesus "is the image of the
invisible God" (Colossians 1:15). Again we recall how the
creation story in Genesis describes all humanity as being
formed in the image and likeness of God, suggesting a
kinship between the divine Spirit or Awareness and the
awareness or spirit of human lives. Jesus, Paul held, in his
life, death, and new life, was a special disclosure of what this
likeness was like. While Paul maintained that "in him all the
fullness of God was pleased to dwell" (Colossians 1:19), he
realized that all of what God must be in order to be God
could only partially be seen in a human life. But Jesus had
been and was this image. He was this *imago Dei*. He was
this parable of God revealing vital insights into God's heart
and ways. The gospel story of the transfiguration, which
describes Jesus' face shining "like the sun" and his garments
becoming "dazzling white," is a glimpse of the divine
beauty being reflected in Jesus' humanity (Matthew 17:2).
All are made in the image of God, but Jesus was unique in
making this likeness visible. He is, as one of the creeds seeks
to express it, the ineffable, "Light from Light," light from
invisible light—invisible light made visible. In the words of
the fourth-century hymn of Bishop Ambrose, which was
set to music in Richard's own years:

O splendor of God's glory bright,
O thou that bringest light from light,

O Light of Light, light's living spring,
O Day, all days illumining.

With friends and colleagues and fellow worshippers
Richard would have sung this hymn to the transcendent
God of all creation, the Son who was God's revelation and
the immanent Spirit of life:

All laud to God the Father be;
all praise eternal Son to thee;
all glory to the Spirit raise
in equal and unending praise. (Hymn 5)

Seeing Jesus

But how could Richard see and know Jesus, who had lived
his human life long ago? How could he (or we) pray to see
him more clearly? Richard would also have remembered
the story of doubting Thomas seeing the risen Jesus. Who
could blame Thomas for questioning Jesus' resurrection?
Surely no one rises from the mighty power of death! *There
must be some mistake—some other explanation.* "Unless I see
the mark of the nails in his hands, and put my finger in the
mark of the nails and my hand in his side, I will not believe"
(John 20:25). Only seeing—and in Thomas's case, only
seeing up close and touching—is believing!

A week later Jesus' disciples were again in the house,
and Thomas was with them. Although the doors
were shut, Jesus came and stood among them and

said, "Peace be with you." Then he said to Thomas, "Put your finger here and see my hands. Reach out your hand and put it in my side. Do not doubt but believe." Thomas answered him, "My Lord and my God!" Jesus said to him, "Have you believed because you have seen me? Blessed are those who have not seen and yet have come to believe." (John 20:26–29)

Richard could not touch or see Jesus as Thomas had done except through the eyes of faith and in the hearing and pondering of the disciples' beliefs and memories. But in that faith a sense of Jesus' presence does not disappear with his death or end with the stories about his physical presence after the resurrection. "I am with you always, to the ends of the age," Jesus promises (Matthew 28:20). Jesus' Spirit, the disciples believe, is yet among them. "Where two or three are gathered in my name, I am there among them" (Matthew 18:20).

Pious Christian may sometimes seem to speak too glibly about Jesus' presence—of "knowing" the Lord, of "seeing" the Savior, of his "walking" and "talking" with them. They are, however, finding their own words for what the early disciples discovered in the Spirit of God, now also recognized by them to be the Spirit of Jesus. This must have been how Paul could claim to have seen the risen Lord and say, "It is no longer I who live, but it is Christ who lives in me" (Galatians 2:20). In John's gospel Jesus encourages his followers with this promise: "The Holy Spirit, whom the Father will send in my name, will teach you everything, and remind you of all that I have said to you. . . . You have heard me say to you, 'I am going away, and I am coming to you.' If you loved me, you would rejoice that I am going to the Father" (John 14:26, 28). In a relationship of love the Father,

the Son, and the Spirit are one. Into that relationship disciples are invited. "As you, Father, are in me and I am in you,
may they also be in us" (John 17:21). "Those who love me
will keep my word, and my Father will love them, and we
will come to them and make our home with them" (John
14:23). Or in the words of the Irish hymn, "Thine own may
I be; thou in my dwelling, and I one with thee." So did
Richard and other Christians with him—and with us—
come to see and know their Lord Jesus.

Keeping Jesus' Word

This knowing and keeping of Jesus' word, Richard learned,
is in the loving of others. "This is my commandment, that
you love one another as I have loved you" (John 15:12).
Such loving involves the giving and sharing of self. "No
one," says Jesus, "has greater love than this, to lay down one's
life for one's friends. You are my friends if you do what I
command you" (John 15:13–14). What Jesus commands is
love: the love of God and the love of one's neighbor as
oneself (Mark 12:29–31). We are to love God by responding
to God's passionate love in Jesus. "We love because God first
loved us" (1 John 4:19), and in this life such love is made
known by loving others as we have been loved. Disciples
cannot claim to love God, "whom they have not seen," if
they do not love their brothers and sisters, "whom they have
seen" (1 John 4:20–21).

This call to "love one another" rings like a bell through the chapters of the new covenant: *one another, one another, one another.* The Greek word is *allelon: allelon, allelon, allelon.*

> I give you a new commandment, that you love one another (*allelon*). Just as I have loved you, you also should love one another. By this everyone will know that you are my disciples, if you have love for one another. (John 13:34–35)

Richard sees in Jesus the love of God and the love that God calls forth in Jesus' followers. This loving must be not just in word, Jesus tells his disciples, but in action:

> Do you know what I have done to you? You call me Teacher and Lord—and you are right, for that is what I am. So if I, your Lord and Teacher, have washed your feet, you also ought to wash one another's (*allelon*) feet. (John 13:12–14)

How do we love God, whom we cannot see? By loving one another—honoring our sisters and brothers, caring for friends and strangers, feeding those who are hungry, and healing those who are sick. "Lord, when was it that we saw you hungry and gave you food, or thirsty and gave you something to drink? And when was it that we saw you a stranger and welcomed you, or naked and gave you clothing? And when was it that we saw you sick or in prison and visited you?" the righteous people in Jesus' parable ask. "Truly I tell you," replies the king, "just as you did it to one of the least of these who are members of my family, you did it to me'" (Matthew 25:31–40).

Seeing like this will always be a challenge. Living with such vision, as was true for Jesus, means living as if loving really matters most, despite all the powers of anxiety's fear and greed and evil to the contrary. We can imagine Richard learning this as he prayed and as he sought, as best he could, to imitate the ways of Jesus. He lived, as we all live, in what has been called a "participatory universe." To understand we must also enter in and experience. It is one thing to observe a forest from afar; it is quite another to walk under its canopies, step over fallen limbs, see squirrels, and hear the birds. We may critique literature, but fully to appreciate it we have also to live in the story. Even the scientist becomes participant in the experiment.

There are measures of objectivity, but in many ways we see what we want to see, and must participate in order to live into what we think we see. But sometimes it is so hard to see what is good—what is of love. One can imagine Richard, not unlike all disciples at least some of the time, feeling that he was like the blind beggar Bartimaeus (Mark 10:46–52). In his darkness Bartimaeus calls out, "Jesus, Son of David, have mercy on me!" Voices tell him to be silent, but more ardently he beseeches, "Son of David, have mercy on me!" Jesus responds to him, "What do you want me to do for you?" "My teacher, let me see again," he replies, and Bartimaeus gains his sight. He is then able to see Jesus, and Mark's gospel tells us that immediately the man who had been blind "followed him on the way." Bartimaeus saw well enough to follow Jesus "on the way" to Jerusalem, "on the way" of love's compassion and the keeping of the commandment to love one another.

Jesus often tells of the blind seeing and the deaf hearing, of ears that will hear and eyes that are blessed to see (Mark 4:9; Matthew 13:16). Such eyes are "the eyes" of an enlightened heart (Ephesians 1:18). Such eyes belong to those who thirst to see God's ways (Psalm 42:2), who want to see the face of God made known in Jesus. If we want to see forgiveness, we must also forgive (Matthew 6: 12, 14). If we want to know love, we must also love.

This love and forgiveness, Richard understood, began with God. Love and forgiveness were made visible in Jesus' love and forgiveness. We can imagine Richard kneeling before a kind of triptych of his threefold prayer to see more clearly, to love more dearly, and to follow more nearly. In the first panel he could now see the love and forgiveness in the bread broken and the wine poured out for all (Mark 14:24; 1 Corinthians 11:24). He could hear forgiveness and love through the Spirit of Jesus, who "will take what is mine and declare it to you" (John 16:15). Jesus is the image through whom the light of divine life is glimpsed. Even in life's dimness—especially in times of darkness—Jesus is the Light from Light. In his evening prayers Richard would sing the ancient hymn:

> O gracious Light, Lord Jesus Christ,
> in you the Father's glory shone.
> Immortal, holy, blest is he,
> and blest are you, his holy Son. (Hymn 25)

We know and see Jesus, Richard came to understand, in our prayer. We know God and we see Jesus on our knees. With Richard we continue to pray for this gracious Light, enabling us to see Jesus more clearly even when times are dim and the future clouded. We can imagine Richard kneeling with his prayer: he bends before his Redeemer Lord, his Brother and Friend, praying in the Garden of Gethsemane, praying from the cross, "Father, forgive them." He hears Jesus calling his disciples to love another "as I have loved you."

Beseeching the Light of minds that praise you, the Life of souls that love you, the Strength of hearts that would

serve you, we, too, may bend the knee of our hearts before
our Friend and God, as in thanksgiving, dear Lord, these
three things of you we pray:

> *to see you more clearly,*
> *to love you more dearly,*
> *to follow you more nearly,*
> *day by day.*

three

TO LOVE YOU
MORE DEARLY

By the year 1235, at the age of thirty-eight, Richard had returned from his studies and teaching abroad. A doctor of canon law, he had now been appointed to be the chancellor—the head and chief canon lawyer—of Oxford University. Although he would have missed friendships and contacts with other universities and the continental church, Richard must have found pleasure in being among former companions again and with the familiar sights of Oxford. He had embarked upon a distinguished academic and administrative career well suited to one ambitious to serve his Lord and church. The recent expansion of canon law meant that a church-administered legal system controlled numerous components of daily life—not only in the strictly religious sphere but also in the "secular" areas of wills, inheritances, marriage dowries, and many other aspects of political and civil life.

Along with his immersion in canon law, Richard would have been interested in related theological issues. There were, at that time, ongoing theological discussions and debate regarding the nature not only of human existence but of reality itself. Subtle but important differences could be found among the positions held by the most prominent medieval theologians. The *realists* were strongly influenced by Plato and his theory of "forms," which held that the pure idea, or essence, of something (the "tableness" of a table or the "donkeyness" of a donkey) is a universal paradigm held in the mind of the Creator and the highest form of reality. These forms are eternal and exist independently of the world of time and space.

This school of thought was opposed to the *nominalist* view, influenced by Aristotelian understandings, which was inclined to focus on the particular—in this case, on the actual table or the actual donkey—rather than on abstract universals. This still-evolving philosophy gave greater prominence to what was individual and distinctive. The development of nominalism would, in time, lead to more scientific ways of thinking and approaches to the world. The dominant philosophical position in Richard's time, however, would have held to the reality of divine ideas, even though qualified by the understanding that there was also a constituent factor that made each member of a group or species individually distinct.

From this distance, to us the largely scholastic and abstract debates may seem rather abstruse and even unimportant. They would have been just as interesting to educated men like Richard, however, as vigorous arguments over the relationship of mind and matter, or about how ideas or *models* relate to the working of things (think of quantum mechanics or string theory) are to many philosophically and

scientifically minded people today. The concern is with the
nature of reality, both seen and unseen. Although knowl-
edgeable about these discussions and debates, Richard
would likely have been content with a position as a kind of
moderate realist. In any case, as one trained in the law, he
had a pragmatic bent of mind that was more interested in
the social and political aspects of life. His theology and faith
in God, one surmises, would have been based more on the
Bible rather than on metaphysics or philosophy.

And the Politics

There was also much going on politically and, given his
prominence, Richard would have found himself in the
thick of struggles among the various factions loyal to King
Henry III of England, the Pope in Rome, and the Archbishop of Canterbury, who was appointed by the Pope as
head over the English church. Only twenty years earlier,
King John, the father of Henry III, had been forced to grant
the *Magna Carta,* a document guaranteeing certain civil and
political rights, including a measure of liberty for the church
in England.

For someone like Richard, deep loyalties would have
remained divided, as was true also internationally: the strong
papacy sometimes favored the king, and at other times
worked against him. To whom did one's chief allegiance
belong, as both an Englishman and a Catholic Christian?
Was it to the king, to the Pope (and sometimes to his legate),
or to the Archbishop of Canterbury, who represented the

Pope but was in service to the king as well? Or did one's chief loyalty belong to the whole people of God, and not least, for reasons we have seen, to the poor—and, within and beyond all other loyalties, to God and God's ways?

As always, politics was enmeshed in personality, power, and finances. Senior church positions controlled considerable amounts of property and money. Who would make appointments to these benefices? To whom would the appointees give their chief support, and with whom would they share revenues? Although many of the circumstances of life in the thirteenth century were different from our own, we can still imagine parallels and similarities with our lives today, as we try to sort out problems, opportunities, loyalties, and allegiances. Then and now, money, revenues, and resources were often the strongest motivating factor in political and church affairs, all denials to the contrary. It is money, after all else is said about it, that gives power over other people's time and labor. Money and resources that rightly belonged to the church were needed for the church's ministries, not least the ministries of charity. No wonder Richard had found himself praying to see and know his Lord and the Lord's ways more clearly.

Soon he would find himself even more deeply caught up in the political struggles. Richard's friend and former teacher, Edmund Rich, was appointed Archbishop of Canterbury in 1233 by Pope Gregory IX. Early in his life Edmund had been known for his austerity and piety; now this somewhat withdrawn and highly ethical man was trying to check both papal exactions and royal mismanagement of funds. He struggled to keep his balance between Henry III and the Pope, striving at the same time to defend his archiepiscopal rights and to stop the exploitation of church wealth and patronage while also supporting efforts for church reform. These efforts put him at odds with both king and Pope.

Edmund asked Richard to be his chancellor and to help him with these tasks and challenges. Indeed, it would seem that Richard came to take on much of the legal and administrative work, while Edmund devoted himself more to prayer and contemplation. The two friends became even closer to one another, suggesting what some have seen as a profound reality of Christian discipleship. Just as Jesus sent forth his disciples in pairs, so in the life of the church saints are often found in pairs, as though God had given them to each other for support in life's struggles.

Exile

The situation, however, became more hard-pressed when Henry III induced the Pope to appoint a cardinal legate who would come to England and settle disputes as the Pope's personal representative. Edmund, marginalized within the power structure and increasingly unwell, found his position as Archbishop untenable and left England in self-imposed exile. Richard went with him to France and sought refuge in a Cistercian abbey in Pontigny, to which earlier Archbishops of Canterbury (Thomas Becket and Stephen Langton) had also repaired when in distress. Edmund died there in 1240, and Richard, now forty-three years old, was left alone, both away from home and out of favor with the royal court.

This must have been a time of sorrow and some despair, during which Richard evidently engaged in periods of fasting and various other austerities. Wearing rough clothing and living frugally, he tried to come to terms with his situation and respond to the love of God by searching for a deeper holiness in his life. He wanted to "put to death" in himself all the "impurity, passion, evil desire, and greed" (Colossians 3:5) that were not of God and that could trick him into losing sight of God's ways. One can imagine him at the time earnestly praying "to love you more dearly" and repeating the psalmist's cry, "O God you are my God; I seek you eagerly; my soul and body thirst for you in barren lands and dry." Then he would pray on:

> Therefore I gazed upon you
>   Within your holy place,
> That I might look upon your power,
>   The glory of your face.
>
> Your love is more than life:
>   My lips shall give you praise:
> I lift my hands up in your Name
>   And bless you all my days.
>
> My soul is well content,
>   My mouth shall give you praise
> When I remember you at night
>   And ponder all your ways.
>
> Your wings have sheltered me,
>   My helper in the past;
> My soul, Lord, clings to you alone,
>   Your right hand holds me fast.
>   (Psalm 63:1–8)[8]

To Be a Priest

It is possible that Richard may have previously felt himself unworthy of priestly ordination. Or perhaps it was more a matter of dedication to his vocation as a canon lawyer. But through his prayers he now determined that he was called to be a preacher and pastor. In this way, he believed, he could best serve God and others. He journeyed to Orleans to take up residence in a Dominican house of studies, there to deepen his theological understandings.

Once again he would have found himself in the midst of the theological debates of the day. In this same decade the young Thomas Aquinas became a Dominican and began writing his *Summa Theologica,* a vast collection of articles intended to systematize and "sum up" all of medieval theology for the Christian believer. What is the nature of God? What is knowledge, and how do we know? What is real in life? What can be learned from the created natural world? What is the relationship between the objects we see in the natural world—a rock, a cloud—and the eternal ideas of rocks and clouds that exist outside of time? What is the relationship between faith and human reason, and between reason and what is revealed in scripture?

Perhaps it was as much through his intuition as through any process of reasoning that Richard came to appreciate what Aquinas and others tried to articulate. Men and women may attempt to think about and imagine the God of all life and being. They can proceed by way of analogy. Human beings, made in the image of God, may through their reasoning gain some insight into divine wisdom. Yet human intelligence is but an imperfect imitation of the divine. Whatever our ideas about God, the lesser still cannot comprehend the greater. The human mind cannot take in the divine. The more such efforts at comprehending God seem to succeed, the more obviously they fail. It is, in fact, easier and perhaps wiser to say what God is *not* than what God *is*. (God cannot be unjust; God cannot be unwise.) The most basic observation we can make about human-scale pictures or images of God is that they are too small—even ludicrously so. It is like our trying to imagine infinity. However clever human beings are, if we try to comprehend God with our limited mental capacities and to "re-size" God for human comprehension, we can be sure of one thing: this is not God. Moreover, attempting to worship or be in relationship with a God who is understood in so limited a fashion could be close to idolatry.

Not to Our Love

A relationship of love, Aquinas recognized, is a different matter. The intellect can help, but the human mind tries to pull God in, as it were, in order to have a conception of the divine. Love, however, reaches out in the direction of relationship. Love attempts to go beyond the self. Love can be in relationship with One greater than oneself. "Only to our intellect is God incomprehensible," wrote the author of *The Cloud of Unknowing* a century later, "not to our love."[9] Love can begin to discern what the intellect by itself cannot imagine. "Here on earth," as Jeremy Taylor, an Anglican of deep and ongoing prayer, wrote in a sermon, "we must first love, and love will open our eyes as well as our hearts, and we shall then see and perceive and understand."[10]

We gain a hint of this kind of understanding in human relationships. Other people can be difficult for us to understand. We may find it hard to appreciate who they are and what their gifts and motives might be. Loving them offers ways of deeper relationship as we reach out beyond our need to know them only for our own wants and purposes.

When we love another individual, we wish to be able to express that love. Because of our insecurities and our desire to have the other person meet our needs, our love often comes with strings attached, and may even be manipulative as we pull on the strings. But we can at least imagine a loving that goes beyond just our own needing and, when we do, then it seems much more a privilege to love. We feel cheated if we cannot offer our love—or if we are not able to try to give it words or set it to song. Richard came to this way of love's understanding, and we hear again his prayer as a hymn, singing, "May I love you more dearly." In every language people of faith sing of this yearning love for God.

Holy, holy, holy,
My heart is glad to say the words:
You are holy, God.

Santo, santo, santo,
mi corazon te adora.
Mi corazon te sabes decir:
Santo eres, Senor.[11]

When I was a young man, I had a hard time understanding what such adoration meant. Somewhere I had been taught that God had created humans in order to receive praise, honor, and worship from them. The picture that formed in my mind was of God riding around in an open car—something like in the newsreels I had seen of President Eisenhower—lifting his arms and signaling for more applause and acclaim. Did God, I wondered, need this? Was this what we were created for?

It took more experience of human love for me to begin to get the idea that the receiving of love is what the beloved does not out of need, but of love. For example, I am sure my mother did not *need* all the drawings, clay knickknacks, and lanyards that I brought home to her as a little boy. Still, they meant something to her and she was kind enough to keep them around for a while, usually on or on top of the refrigerator. I doubt whether God needs our songs and prayers. I like to think, however, that in the relationship of love God may get a charge out of them even if they are mostly for us—so that we can reach beyond ourselves.

It has been observed that people all wrapped up in themselves make pretty small packages. In love's worship we can begin to unwrap ourselves, to open and grow into what John Donne called our "abler selves." That is what worship at its best is about: individuals and communities who are not centering their thoughts so much on them-selves, but are instead giving thanks for life and offering, as best they can, their love. In its more intense modes such adoration becomes ecstatic. This adoration is loving God "with all your heart, and with all your soul, and with all your mind, and with all your strength." The companion commandment offers the insight that those "abler selves"— no longer so self-centered—will also be able to begin to "love your neighbor as yourself" (Mark 12:30–31).

Ecstasy comes from two Greek words: *stasis,* which means "to stand" or "to be," and *ek,* which can mean "out of" or "outside of." In experiences of strong emotion one steps outside life's lesser concerns and the tendency to be preoccupied with self. Usually we think of such ecstasy as relatively momentary—intense joy and love that then pass away as we return to our more mundane tasks and preoccupied lives. But love's worship also offers the opportunity of a more steady state of *ek-stasis,* of reaching beyond self and of living beyond narrow self-interest. Then we may come to care about God and God's ways more consistently—day by day. Then it is that God, in the relationship of love, can begin to live in and through our inadequate ideas and imaginings of all that God might be. This was the intention of Richard's prayer when he asked to "love you more dearly."

Toward You

The heart, however, as Richard would have read in the *Confessions* of Saint Augustine, remains "restless until it rests in you"—or "toward you" (*ad te*)—in relationship.[12] We do not find an end to our restlessness in this life, but we may find the beginning of this end when in love's worship and prayer we go outside or beside ourselves. And for Richard, as we have seen, relationship with God found its most intimate expression in his sense of kinship with the living presence of God in Jesus. This is how he could best know and love God.

His love for Jesus, as the movement of Richard's three
petitions suggests, is the centerpiece of the triptych of his
prayer: seeing, loving, and following. A triptych is a painting
on three panels that are joined by hinges, so that the two
sides can fold over the central panel. With love as the
centerpiece, the eyes of faith may move back and forth from
knowing the Lord more clearly and to following more
nearly by and through loving more dearly. Love is the heart
of the relationship. Without love, as Paul put it, all other
skills and talents make one but "a noisy gong or a clanging
cymbal" (1 Corinthians 13:1), for "the only thing that
counts is faith working through love" (Galatians 5:6). Love,
reaching out beyond self, is enabled to see and follow more
nearly. And here, at the heart of knowing and following, the
soul of our human awareness finds at least a measure of
contentment in recognizing its deepest desire. It rests in the
love and loving of the beloved. It knows that there is no
other way of knowing and wishes to follow in the way that
there is no other way of going.

Letting go, quieting down from anxiety and competi-
tiveness, the loving heart may for a time have no further
need of words. There may arise the silence of lovers who
have done all they can to express and embody their love.
No more is needed. Love is in the silence. Love *is* the
silence. Such loving silence seems the keenest adoration, full
of harmony and love's peace.

Sheer Silence

Richard would have remembered how the prophet Elijah, deeply troubled in the circumstances of his life and calling, realized God's presence. He found God's Spirit not in the wind, not in the earthquake, nor in the fire, but in "a sound of sheer silence" (1 Kings 19:11–12). Yet Richard may also in his prayers have realized, and I will confess realizing as well, how intensely *silent* that sheer silence can be. Perhaps we all have experienced times when the silence may seem to empty out. We may feel loneliness. We may even be afraid. Perhaps, we wonder, if in love's ecstasy we have let go too far beyond our self-interest and self-love. Perhaps, in a long prayer of silence, we find ourselves asking, *What's in it for me?* Am I not at this point supposed to feel more fulfilled rather than emptied out? Is not prayer and religion meant, at least in some measure, to act as a form of therapy to make myself feel better about myself? With such thoughts we rise off the knees of our heart and turn away from the prayer of seeking "to love you more dearly." We may retreat to more familiar or perhaps to new religious words and practices as a way of filling up and ending the silence—and any ecstasy. More likely, given the thoroughly secular people we are, we find distractions in work or amusements, and crave the company and conversation of others.

Now, surely friendship, work, and recreation can be healthy. They are all part of the good balance of a life lived for self, God, and others. In them we may continue to live for love of God, others, and self. But the insecurities of our fears and loneliness may also preoccupy us, keeping us from relationships of caring and love. Martin Luther spoke of the human tendency to be *incurvatus in se*—to be "curved in upon the self," wrapped up in the self, which as we know makes for a pretty small package.

In my urge to end or fill up the silence with my own diversions I may plunge into my work or recreation so as to exhaust any other hopes. Anxious over my incompleteness and mortality, I may consume with abandon. "In the shadow of the hawk," Edna St. Vincent Millay observed, "we feather our nests."[13] In my fear that I am wasting my life and am myself wasting away, I seek more ways of *killing* time. I may come to dread giving Jesus access to my deepest heart and, through my distractions, try to avoid my own "abler self" as well.

I imagine that Richard must have known such fears and anxieties as part of the human condition. He would not have had available all of the distractions and indulgences we have today at our fingertips but, like every human being, he would have had his own ways of escaping. His major response, however, seems to have taken the form of more intense piety and reverential activity, including his fasting, rough clothing, and other deprivations. There is little doubt that Richard would have had a lively fear of hell, and, in any case, he was trying to avoid the hell of God's disfavor. Maybe, he worried, his present circumstances as an exile without royal or ecclesiastical favor were already forms of God's punishment. Where was God's forgiveness? Where was God's love? Where was God in the silence? Why was God so silent? "Why, O LORD, do you stand far off? Why do you hide yourself in times of trouble?" (Psalm 10:1).

Love's Skin

Scripture tells us that "we love because God first loved us" (1 John 4:19). We can love because of God's love already in the world. We are capable of love because a loving God has taken the initiative. But where and how is this love shown to us? Perhaps one can say that it is in the creation of life and especially of human life that God's love is shown. For our bodies and spirits, for reason, thinking, and awareness, for music and all the beauties of the world we may offer our love's gratitude. Days come, however, when the idea of creative love may seem too abstract in a world that is a mixture of good and evil, of pleasures, beauties, sorrows, and suffering. A creator God may seem far away.

We can understand the little girl who, one thundering and sky-flashing night, wanted to crawl into her mother's bed. "Don't worry, darling," her mother said. "You don't need to be afraid. God loves you." "I know," the child fretted through her tears, "but tonight I need some skin." The capacity for love may come from God, but we pray, too, that we can find also find love's "skin" in our lives, loves, and friendships.

Richard had known love with his brother and sister, with friends like Edmund and Ralph Bocking and later Simon and William, but the chief story of love for his life was the parable of God's love embodied in Jesus. Jesus had experienced the love of God in his own human life. He called upon God as a father and spoke of God's parent-like love. Jesus taught his disciples to pray, "Father, hallowed be

your name" (Luke 11:2). He was remembered to have used
an Aramaic word, *Abba,* which, just like our words "mama"
and "dada," derived from a child's early word for father.
"Abba," he prayed in the Garden of Gethsemane on the
night before his death (Mark 14:36). The Aramaic word
seems to have continued in use even in the Greek-language
prayers of the early disciples who, when they cried, *"Abba,*
Father," knew the Spirit of God and of Christ Jesus present
with their spirits (Romans 8:15–16).

Jesus told a parable of a father who was eager to forgive
and reconcile both the son who wasted his inheritance and
the elder son who remained grudging and self-righteous.
He told other surprising stories. A shepherd went to
extraordinary lengths to rescue one lost sheep. Laborers
who worked for only an hour in the late afternoon were
paid the same wage as those who started at sunrise. A
Samaritan, member of a despised minority, stopped to help
someone beaten by robbers after the more respectable had
passed him by. Jesus, moreover, was seen as the principal
actor in stories of healing and reaching out to those otherwise thought to be lost and beyond God's care. He *bodied
forth* God's goodness and love to the sick, those beaten up,
the outcast, and the lonely. Finally, he was willing to give his
life for these others. There is no "greater love than this, to
lay down one's life for one's friends" (John 15:13). This was
God's love in human skin—in human flesh and life.

The central panel of Richard's prayer triptych was
embellished with these pictures of God's love in Jesus: Jesus
himself as the good shepherd and the good Samaritan,
healing Bartimaeus, feeding the five thousand, cleansing a
leper, talking with the woman at the well, eating with Levi
and Zacchaeus. But always in the center of the panel was
Jesus on the cross, sharing in all the pain, the grief, and the

cruelty of life. With his arms outstretched, he was seeking to reconcile and invite each of us into a new relationship of love with God. We can even imagine inscribed beneath the central panel of Richard's triptych these verses from one of Paul's letters:

> For while we were still weak, at the right time Christ died for the ungodly. Indeed, rarely will anyone die for a righteous person—though perhaps for a good person someone might actually dare to die. But God proves his love for us in that while we still were sinners Christ died for us. (Romans 5:6–8)

First a Child

The healing love that Paul describes in this letter to the Romans had first come into flesh and mortal life wordlessly and wondrously in the skin of a baby—an infant who calls forth our protective care and healing. A ninth-century hymn Richard would have known tells the story:

> Creator of the stars of night,
> your people's everlasting light,
> O Christ, Redeemer of us all,
> we pray you hear us when we call.

> When this old world drew on toward night,
> you came; but not in splendor bright,
> not as a monarch, but the child
> of Mary, blameless mother mild. (Hymn 60)

Richard would also have prayed to Jesus' mother, the
Mother of God, "Mary, blameless, mother mild." She, after
all, had foretold and joined in her Son's prophetic ministry
by praising the God who "has brought down the powerful
from their thrones, and lifted up the lowly." She too knew
the God who "has filled the hungry with good things, and
sent the rich away empty" (Luke 1:52–53). Her son then
healed the sick and welcomed sinners. He challenged those
who wanted to keep God's care only for themselves, as the
righteous and rewarded in this life. He invited the sick and
the well, the sinful and the righteous into a new community of reconciling love. Finally, he gave himself to suffering
and crucifixion. "Thanks be to you, my Lord Jesus Christ,"
Richard prayed, "for all the benefits which you have given
me, for all the pains and insults you have borne for me, O
most merciful Redeemer, Friend, and Brother." In Jesus,
God was friend and brother to Richard. "May I love you
more dearly."

We are once more surprised and awed by God's love in
Jesus. Could it really be that the God who is the "Creator
of the stars of night" and of all that lives has shown such
love? Could it be that the God of all that is cares so for us?
Does God care so much for me? Does God care for me
with my good moments, but also all my *stuff*—addictive
distractions, coping habits, and living so closely guarded
within myself, so wrapped up? Could I be loveable?

Richard's fasting and the hairshirts may have had their
purposes in disciplining selfishness, but he might also have
wondered, *in what measure are they really needed, my merciful
Redeemer, Friend, and Brother?* Love comes without merit.
God's love in Jesus comes to us first—while we are still
wrapped in selfishness. God's love in Jesus helps us to know
that we are loved and loveable and then able to unwrap and

reach out with love's response. In the mystery of relationship, love, to be known as love, needs a response. Love,
Richard would have discovered, is unknown except in the
loving, while there is no other condition or requirement.
One finds one is loveable by being loved. Healed by love
from guilt, anxiety, and insecurity's greed, those who find
themselves loved by God in Jesus are love-able—able to
respond and to offer love in a relationship of love.

And One Another

As we have become love-able, so we are able, as the
commandment tells us, to offer healing and love to our
neighbors—all those to whom we can express love. We are
able to love them as we are loved and to love them as
ourselves. Knowing forgiveness and kindness, knowing
ourselves loved and loving ourselves, we are to share in this
care with and for others.

   There are grounds, of course, for saying that it is not
possible to love in ways that go beyond some form of self-
interest. Many sociobiologists and psychologists argue that
human beings, like all other animals, can live only self-
interested lives. There are certainly dangers in denying the
significance of self-interest in all our activities. Like other
animals, however, we may do sacrificial acts that benefit the
health and continuation of the species or clan. The "golden
rule" of doing to others as one would have them do to us
can be understood as a sophisticated self-interested way of
contributing to a common good in which one may share

benefits with others. And what a highly developed good that can become through the practice of thinking of others' needs and opportunities! And just maybe, with the experience and practice of love, in the ecstasy of the beauty of God's loving and compassion, there can evolve a human love in which we are not at the center but more fully members of a community of mutual responsibility and love.

"If I am not for myself, who will be?" asked a rabbi long ago. But, he went on, "If I am only for myself, who am I?" We are given ourselves to love and be loved and are not much good to anyone else without love. On the other hand, if all we can do is consider our own well-being, that is a fair definition of immaturity. Probably we could all agree that an immature person is someone who seems unable to take into account any other needs than his or her own. Curved in and wrapped up in self, the true narcissist, as the story goes, says, "Well, that's enough about me. Now tell me about you. What do you think of me?"

The "abler self" is able to walk in another's shoes. One who knows love can empathize and share compassion. That is why Jesus offers the story of the shepherd seeking the one who is lost, and tells of a father who loves both his sons, one lost to prodigality and the other to self-righteousness. The parent continues to love both children into a new kind of family. Seeking to draw his disciples beyond their self-centeredness, Jesus tells them that in caring for those in need, for those without enough to live decently—those without power or status in society, including the sick, the stranger, the hungry, and those in prison—they are caring for him (Matthew 25:35–40). Richard would have understood that in trying to offer care for the least in the world, he was loving more dearly his Lord who had come "not to be served but to serve" (Mark 10:45).

Again, we hear the call of the bell of love for one another ringing throughout the new covenant. In still more words of Jesus and his disciples, one hears its pealing and promise:

> This is my commandment, that you love one another (*allelon*) as I have loved you. No one has greater love than this—to lay down one's life for one's friends. You are my friends if you do what I command you. (John 15:12–14)

> God has so arranged the body... that there may be no dissension within the body, but the members may have the same care for one another (*allelon*). If one member suffers, all suffer together with it. (1 Corinthians 12:24–26)

> ... through love be servants of one another (*allelon*). (Galatians 5:13, RSV)

Both being loved and loving others as Jesus has loved us can become a kind of rhythm of life. There is music in "Love your neighbor / as yourself" and "Love one another / as I have loved you." It is a rhythm that one might imagine as a dance, first one foot and then the other—the self being loved along with the other, both then moving together to make the dance of loving and being loved.

Enough?

Many of us, however, understandably become anxious about scarcities in life: not enough time, not enough money or security or clean air or time off. For too many people, food, good water, and housing are in short supply. We may worry, too, that there will not be enough love to go around. Then we think we had better be careful with it—who gets love, and how much? For some people, dealing with this anxiety may seem to be what religion is all about. *If I am unsure of the love of God and whether there is enough for me, let's be sure no one else has any more.* Perhaps the anxiety comes from the uncertainties of childhood, when we are never sure whether our parents love us more or less than our brothers and sisters, and we are worried there may not be enough love to go around.

Genuine loving, however, works by a different arithmetic. It is more like a muscle being well exercised. The more it is strengthened, the more strength there is to use. Such seems to have been the theme in several of Jesus' stories about God's ways: there is more than enough to go around. In a number of Jesus' parables and in the stories of the feeding of the multitudes and the turning of water into wine at the wedding, there is abundance—even extravagance. At least as far as God's love is concerned, there is no shortage. The more the love is responded to and exercised, the more there is to share.

Schooled as we also are by our insecurities, such abundance may seem hard to believe and trust in. We feel the need to guard love just as we do everything else. If we love others too much, it will make us vulnerable, and there may not be enough for ourselves. If we try to love God with all our heart, soul, mind, and strength, what will be left for us? The promise of God's love makes, of course, for nice words! The invitation to live as if love matters most offers a marvelous adventure! But it can seem frightening, too.

Richard must have known this fear and anxiety as he studied to be a priest and wondered about his future ministry. Still in exile, he would have asked, "What is going to happen to me?" Perhaps in hesitation his journeying soul "drew back," in the words of George Herbert's poem "Love," for he knew he was "guilty of dust and sin."[14] He may have feared he was a guest unworthy of his Lord's love. How, with all these uncertainties, could he genuinely love others and his God? How should he love his Lord?

No Sweeter Sound

Richard looked again at the central panel of his life of prayer and meditation. There was Jesus reaching out to him. There was Jesus, who had called him friend, laying down his life for him. There he hung both in desperate human need while giving himself in love. Here was love enough. Here was a wealth of love. Jesus, Lord of his heart, was near and dear to him again, and perhaps the words of Saint Patrick's hymn were on his lips:

Christ be with me, Christ within me,
Christ behind me, Christ before me,
Christ beside me, Christ to win me,
Christ to comfort and restore me. (Hymn 370)

Richard knelt. His response of love would echo the words
of another hymn written but a few decades earlier:

Jesus, the very thought of thee
with sweetness fills the breast;
but sweeter far thy face to see,
and in thy presence rest.

No voice can sing, no heart can frame,
nor can the memory find,
a sweeter sound than Jesus' Name,
the savior of mankind.

O hope of every contrite heart,
O joy of all the meek,
to those who fall, how kind thou art:
how good to those who seek!

But what to those who find?
Ah, this nor tongue nor pen can show;
the love of Jesus, what it is,
none but who love him know. (Hymn 642)

On his knees, Richard could know God's love and give
thanks to his Redeemer. In the love of his Friend and
Brother, Richard experienced the hope and the courage to
love others as Jesus had loved him. From the central panel
of his prayer, Jesus reached out to him with the bread of his
life. Finding himself dignified by such love, Richard was
now a guest at table with Jesus, "worthy to be here." Finding
himself loveable, he became able to love and to pray, as we

now do with him: that we may "see you more clearly and
follow you more nearly," and that we may "love you more
dearly, day by day."

four

TO FOLLOW YOU
MORE NEARLY

After further study at the Dominican house in Orleans, Richard was ordained priest by the Bishop of Orleans and made a solemn vow to enter the Dominican order. It seems to have been his plan to give himself to God as a parish priest or perhaps a mendicant teacher and preacher for the rest of his days. Possibly, he thought, in this way he would someday be able to return to England and there serve God and God's people, especially the poor and unfortunate. It was also his hope to spend more of his time in prayer and contemplation. He would take as his own the Dominican motto *contemplata allis tradere,* "to bring to others from contemplation." His life of prayer had deepened. In the midst of such uncertainty, perhaps it was in those years that he began regularly to go to his prayers "even before the birds had begun to sing." Perhaps he prayed with thoughts similar to the prayer the contemplative Thomas

Merton would later offer in an eloquent testament to both
faith and uncertainty:

> My Lord God, I have no idea where I am going. I do
> not see the road ahead of me. I cannot know for
> certain where it will end. Nor do I really know
> myself, and the fact that I think that I am following
> your will does not mean that I am actually doing so.
> But I believe that the desire to please you does in
> fact please you. And I hope I have that desire in all
> that I am doing. I hope that I will never do anything
> apart from that desire. And I know that if I do this
> you will lead me by the right road though I may
> know nothing about it.[15]

Times and politics changed, however, and Richard was
finally able to come back to England and serve as the vicar
of a village church not far from Canterbury. Here he would
have been content to live out his life and ministry. But allegiances continued to shift, and the church soon needed his
talents and devotion in other ways. Boniface, the new Archbishop of Canterbury, asked Richard to join him as his
chancellor and serve him as he had formerly served
Edmund Rich.

In the meantime, a struggle was forming over who
would be the next bishop of the important see of Chichester. The majority of the canons had put Richard forward
to be their bishop, but several local canons who were influenced by King Henry named Robert Passelewe, a royal
clerk, instead. Henry quickly gave his assent, but when
Archbishop Boniface and Robert Grosseteste, Richard's
former teacher and bishop of the large see of Lincoln,
examined Passelewe, they found his credentials lacking and
refused to consecrate him. Boniface now wanted Richard

to be the Bishop of Chichester and gained Pope Innocent IV's agreement, while Chichester's cathedral chapter continued to support Richard's election. King Henry was furious: he remembered the problems he had had with Richard when he was Archbishop Edmund's chancellor. The king refused to accept the election and made it clear that he would prevent Richard from entering his cathedral city. In the meantime, the king was glad to take advantage of the dispute by keeping the revenues from the cathedral and diocese and spending them on his own royal projects.

Once again, Richard was caught between loyalties, including his sense of duty to the Archbishop of Canterbury and his plan to become a Dominican. The Pope sought to resolve his dilemma: he absolved Richard from his vows, and, in 1245, when Richard was forty-eight years old, ordained him as Bishop of Chichester.

Now what was Richard to do? He was a bishop, but Henry had posted a guard and still refused to let him enter the cathedral or town, much less to have access to any of the revenues or powers of the see of Chichester. Richard took up residence in Tarring, a village just sixteen miles from Chichester but in the neighboring diocese of Canterbury. There he lived for the better part of two years with an indigent parish priest by the name of Simon, and did what he could for the local people and clergy of his diocese. He would go on walking tours to nearby villages in his diocese. Friends and supporters helped him to gain a meager living. He became known as a bishop to the poor and was remembered for his own acceptance of poverty and his cheerfulness in the face of life's ups and downs. He felt himself to be living out the heart of what he had learned and taught from canon law and ministering more like the impecunious preaching and teaching friar he had wanted to be.

Following Jesus

In this period of his life Richard would have thought of the apostle Paul, who also tried to follow Jesus in the way of lowliness and service. "Let the same mind be in you that was in Christ Jesus," Paul taught: "Do nothing from selfish ambition or conceit, but in humility regard others as better than yourselves. Let each of you look not to your own interests, but to the interests of others" (Philippians 2:3–5). Honoring oneself and accepting honor from others may be the way of this world, but Jesus' followers, Paul had to remind the new disciples at Corinth over and again, are called to follow a different path. They are to imitate their Lord Jesus: "Though he was rich, yet for your sakes he became poor" (2 Corinthians 8:9). They are to give honor to others rather than seeking their own. In this they many find joy and peace, even if tribulation and disrepute may also be their lot. But it is then that the power of God's love can come to full strength, as surprisingly and wondrously, that "power is made perfect in weakness." All that has turned to love will last and endure. "Therefore," Paul wrote, "I am content with weaknesses, insults, hardships, persecutions, and calamities for the sake of Christ; for whenever I am weak, then I am strong" (2 Corinthians 12:9–10).

Still, the path ahead for Richard was unclear. Again he could pray, "I do not see the road ahead of me." All he could do was to try to follow Jesus—to walk in his way and pray, like Merton, "I believe that the desire to please you does in fact please you. And I hope I have that desire in all that I am doing." Some evenings, after he had returned from his visitations to villages in his diocese, he and Simon may have knelt together and prayed. Seeking to follow more nearly by loving more dearly, they would sing the ancient evening hymn:

> O gracious Light, Lord Jesus Christ,
> in you the Father's glory shone.
> Immortal, holy, blest is he,
> and blest are you, his holy Son.
>
> Now sunset comes, but light shines forth,
> the lamps are lit to pierce the night.
> Praise Father, Son, and Spirit: God
> who dwells in the eternal light.
>
> Worthy are you of endless praise,
> O Son of God, Life-giving Lord;
> wherefore you are through all the earth
> and in the highest heaven adored. (Hymn 25)

Bishop of Chichester

Finally, however, after almost two years and threats of excommunication from Pope Innocent, King Henry relented and allowed Richard to be installed in Chichester Cathedral and assume the administration and revenues of his diocese. Although Chichester was not among the richest dioceses, still Richard's circumstances now changed considerably. He became an eminent figure with a fine cathedral, a household, manor lands, bailiffs, chaplains, and servants at his disposal. But with his position came also many responsibilities. The bishop appointed persons to administer the lands and holdings of the diocese, so many clerics and others now depended on Richard's abilities and integrity as a chief administrator. He needed to build up depleted endowments and to adjudicate disputes over tithes and rights of church patronage.

As bishop, Richard adjusted the revenues of parish churches and regulated the relationships with local monasteries. He worked hard to restore order and morality in his diocese and to discipline but also support the clergy, especially those living in poverty. He was said to be "stiff" with those who insulted his clergy; and he sought to better their education, while also founding a hospital for aged priests. Members of the Dominican and Franciscan orders were deployed for some of the pastoral work. Richard was remembered for taking many funeral services and (one imagines him still physically strong into middle age) often picking up a shovel to help with the burials.

Richard himself continued to live austerely. He disliked ostentation and display and dressed and ate simply. In 1247 there was a severe famine, and the bishop, remembering all he had learned about justice for the poor and seeking to follow his Lord, sold off much of his silver plate to aid the most destitute of his diocese. His greatest authority as bishop, he realized, was a servant authority, following Jesus who, "taking the form of a slave, . . . humbled himself and became obedient to the point of death" (Philippians 2:7–8).

When his love of giving things away distressed his stewards and bailiffs, he told them to "cheer up," reminding them, "We still have enough to live on." When entering a village, he would ask the priest for the names of any who were poor or sick in the parish so he could go to them with gifts of food or money. A strict disciplinarian Richard may have been, especially when it came to injustices and laxness in the church, but the other side of his personality must have also shone through, since he was known, we remember, as "jolly, warm-hearted, courteous, and of a cheerful countenance." People remarked on his kindness to those who had previously opposed him as he sought reconciliation and restored persons who had been excommunicated. However intelligent and well-educated he was, Richard understood that his people would not care how much he knew until they knew how much he cared.

Right Following

Richard's role in political life, meanwhile, remained complex. Medieval church leaders like Richard were often under papal pressure to support and raise money for the series of crusades that sought to restore Jerusalem and the Holy Land to Christian control from the eleventh to the thirteenth centuries. Many people in England opposed such crusades, if for no other reason than that they were expensive and were often waged more in support of papal claims than for any other purpose.

At first Richard, along with Robert Grosseteste and other bishops, stood in opposition to the seventh crusade, but he was appointed by the Pope to preach it and by the court to raise money for it. He may well have recognized this "Christian patriotism" and warmongering for what it was—kings, knights, and members of the aristocracy out for their own pious glory, parading east behind the banner of the cross while benefiting from the rich spoils. Yet, out of his loyalty to the Pope and in the belief that such efforts could help rescue beleaguered Christians in the Holy Land, Richard finally gave his support. Human motivations are regularly mixed; in his way and in his time, Richard was yet trying to follow what he hoped was the will of God.

Then, as now, the will of God was not always easy to discern. Richard spent much of his life torn between wanting a more contemplative life of prayer and being called to active ministries of service. He needed the prayer. He was aware how readily leaders could be caught up in mixed motivations while trying to build up and defend the church. Like many a saint before and after him, Richard likely had a kind of love/hate relationship with the church. He *hated* (in the biblical sense of hating all that does not put God's love first) the church's self-serving and sometimes dissembling ways. Yet he *loved* the church's Lord and so much of the worship, caring, and service offered by the body of Christ. Richard believed that he could most nearly follow the will of God through his ministries to those in need, by his efforts to edify and educate Christians, and by his support of the morality and integrity of the Christian witness. In the church as the body of Christ he could strive to live in imitation of his Lord Jesus in his own humility and austerity, so that he could be a better friend to the lowly and those in greatest need.

We have recognized that Richard's circumstances differed considerably from our own. Yet, as in Richard's life and vocation there must have been days of uncertainty, so in ours there are times of obscurity with regard to God's will—even of darkness. It is hard to see very clearly, much less very far ahead. We may want to live a life of love, but yet we feel our love is weak. Service to our institutions may seem in vain. On many a day all we seem to be able to do is put one foot in front of the other. There is so much to do just to keep our lives going. Any grand vision or high motivation appears to fail us. Our following is haphazard. We plod on, trying as best we can to do our duty of love and care for others. Sometimes it may mean only a step forward and then at least a half-step back. Some days it may feel no more than walking in place.

While it may not seem heroic, such plodding along may in fact not be bad day-by-day guidance and prayer. In its way, it may make for a good theology. Sometimes we are taught that we must first clarify our understandings and motivations. We need to get our theology and worship of God correct; then right behavior will follow. Then we will be *orthodox*; that is, we will practice the right worship and service of God. There is value in this insight but, as we need often to hold in mind, seeing more clearly, loving more dearly, and following more nearly are all part of one prayer. The petitions are closely entwined, and we may pray them in any order.

There are times when trying to follow more nearly may also be the best way to seek to love more dearly and to see and know more clearly. We strive to put the ways of love and love's justice first—to live as if love matters most. Even if on a particular day clear sight or dear loving seem out of reach, we can still try to go by the ways of love and right living. Once again, "the only thing that counts is faith working though love" (Galatians 5:6). This *orthopraxy* is the "right practice" of living. We pray that this kind of living can help to bring about clearer vision and the strength to love the Lord more dearly.

We learn from the liberation theologians that the first
step of love is hungering for and practicing the ways of
love's justness and fairness to the poor and marginalized.
The more we follow this path, the more we learn about
love and the will of God. The learning and the loving are
realized in what Paul calls the "fruit of the Spirit": "love,
joy, peace, patience, kindness, generosity, faithfulness, gentleness, and self-control" of one's own passions and ambitions
(Galatians 5:22–23). Richard would have believed that these
were the signs of the Spirit's presence, while also knowing
many tough days when he could only try as best he could
to follow in the Spirit's ways of faith. Perhaps he would have
recognized the yearning for the fruits of the Spirit heard in
this prayer that echoes the spirituality and life of Francis of
Assisi, another disciple who strove to follow Jesus' Spirit and
who had died only a few years earlier.

> Lord, make us servants of your peace:
> where there is hate, may we sow love;
> where there is hurt, may we forgive;
> where there is strife, may we make one.
>
> Where all is doubt, may we sow faith;
> where all is gloom, may we sow hope;
> where all is night, may we sow light;
> where all is tears, may we sow joy.
>
> Jesus, our Lord, may we not seek
> to be consoled, but to console,
> nor look to understanding hearts,
> but look for hearts to understand.
>
> May we not look for love's return,
> but seek to love unselfishly,

for in our giving we receive,
and in forgiving are forgiven. (Hymn 593)

Arms Out

Richard gazed into the third panel of his prayer triptych. There he saw Jesus gesturing with his arms out to Levi, to James and John, to Peter and Andrew, to Bartimaeus, to Mary Magdalene and Zacchaeus: "Come, follow me." Richard could imagine the Spirit of Jesus similarly reaching out to him. Jesus' first and last words to his disciples in the gospels are, "Follow me" (Mark 1:17; John 21:22). *Follow me in the kingdom of God. Follow me in the ways of God. Follow me in the mystery of discovering your "abler self" and by not putting yourself first.* "Take my yoke upon you, and learn from me," Jesus tells them, "for I am gentle and humble in heart" (Matthew 11:29). Jesus comes among the disciples "as one who serves" (Luke 22:27). "If any want to become my followers," he declares, "let them deny themselves and take up their cross daily and follow me" (Luke 9:23).

When the blind beggar Bartimaeus received his sight from Jesus, he was able to do what disciples often find it hard to do. When he saw more clearly, Bartimaeus was able to follow Jesus "on the way" of faith, on the road to Jerusalem and love's passion. To love as Jesus loves means to go by the way of love's compassion and to be willing to share with Jesus in the passion and suffering of others. Only so can love's true measure be realized.

We must remember that, even in some of his more difficult years, Richard was remembered for his cheerfulness.
He knew the joy of sharing in Jesus' love with others. Yet
the following of Jesus day by day had to be challenging as
well. The opening of one's arms in Jesus' gesture of acceptance of others makes one vulnerable. The gesture can be
risky, as it was for Jesus, whose open arms were subject to
criticism with regard to the kind of people he welcomed
and ate with. Finally, those arms were nailed open on a
cross. Again we realize that in following Jesus our love must
go by the way of compassion—the way of sympathy and
of suffering with others when they are in difficulty. One is
called to seek to transform suffering and sorrow by sharing
in them in love.

The Letter to the Hebrews describes Jesus as "a fore-
runner on our behalf" (6:20), the "pioneer and perfecter of
our faith" who was himself made "perfect through sufferings" (12:2, 2:10). In his human life Jesus was and is out in
front of his followers, a pioneer in the adventure of life.
Those who would follow him come to grow in their own
"abler selves." They leave behind the immaturity of thinking
only of themselves and grow to the maturity that takes into
account the needs and opportunities of others. They reach
out and expand in sympathy and compassion. Knowledge,
together with such compassion, makes for wisdom. Wisdom
is able to understand and value the lives of others. Those
who would follow more nearly the pioneer Jesus want to
grow in this Christian wisdom and come to their full
human stature, "to maturity, to the measure of the full
stature of Christ" (Ephesians 4:13).

Acolytes and Ambassadors

"Follow me," Richard heard Jesus calling to his disciples and to him. *Follow me in God's ways of love and service to others.* From the Greek word for "to follow" *(akoloutheo)* comes our word acolyte. It would seem that being an acolyte is the most fundamental and important office in the community of Jesus. An acolyte is an *attendant*—a follower who gives heed and pays attention in order to learn and to serve. An acolyte is a kind of apprentice. Richard prayed to be such an apprentice and acolyte. "May I follow you more nearly." By doing so, he believed, he would also come to "love you more dearly" and "see you more clearly."

Whether we are a Peter, Zacchaeus, Mary Magdalene, or Bartimaeus, whether we are a fisherman, tax collector, teacher, day laborer, student, or lawyer, each of us is different, with different gifts and experiences. Every disciple prays, each in his or her own way, to become together more like Christ. We pray to be in the imitation of Christ by following him more nearly. Few of us, by God's mercy, will know anything like death on a cross. Jesus has done that for us. But we may yet share in the compassion of his love for others. We may know ourselves so loved that we may "love one another as I have loved you" (John 15:12). Losing self-centered ego in his prayer, Richard would again have echoed Paul's ecstasy: "It is no longer I who live, but it is Christ who lives in me. And the life I now live in the flesh I live by faith in the Son of God, who loved me and gave himself for me" (Galatians 2:20).

When I was a young priest, I went to call on members
of the congregation on one warm summer afternoon. At
one of the homes a four-year-old boy tugged open the
door and stared up at me. I knew Billy from the Sunday
school class of the church. Wide-eyed and without turning
his head, Billy called out to his mother, "Mom, Jesus is
here."

I heard a faint exclamation of surprise as Billy's mother,
a bit flustered and disheveled, came around the corner from
the kitchen, where she had been engaged in some chore.
Billy gave my leg a hug, and his mother and I chuckled
before we sat down to talk about church and family matters.
Later, I thought more about her reaction in that moment
after Billy's announcement and before she reached the door.
Perhaps she knew those passages from the Bible about the
Lord's sudden return. "You do not know when the master
of the house will come, in the evening, or at midnight, or
at cockcrow, or at dawn" (Mark 13:35). I also thought about
my own reaction to being called "Jesus." "Well, I'm certainly
not Jesus," I laughed ruefully, "and not even very good at
being Jesus-like." But then, I thought, are we not all
supposed to try, in our own variety of ways, to be Jesus to
one another as we pray to follow him more nearly?

Desmond Tutu has often reminded us that all Christians
carry Jesus' reputation with them in their hands. People will
come to understand who Jesus is by his followers. Paul says
that disciples are "ambassadors for Christ, since God is
making his appeal through us" (2 Corinthians 5:20). We are
representatives of God's reconciling love in Christ. We may
feel ourselves only novices at this representative work, but
at least we have begun. With these challenging words Teresa
of Avila is said to have described our ministries as acolytes
and ambassadors:

Christ has no body now on earth but yours;
No hands but yours;
No feet but yours:
Yours are the eyes through which Christ's
  compassion looks out into the world;
Yours are the feet with which he is to go
  about doing good;
Yours are the hands with which he is to bless now.

Apprentices

In his heart Richard seems to have intuited this understanding of following and representing Jesus—of trying to
live in the image of God by loving and imitating the one in
whom that image had been best known. Some days we may
not want to see more clearly. Our desire to love more dearly
may slacken. It may seem that in comparison to the love of
Jesus—and in comparison to other disciples as well—we
are just limping along. Still, in our own best way, we can
limp along following Jesus. We can at least keep on trying
to "walk the talk" in embodying the love of God in Jesus.
With the eyes of our hearts enlightened by love's compassion, our mouths may tell of forgiveness and understanding.
Our feet may take us to places where courage and love are
called for, as we reach out our hands in blessing.

On many days I may not feel like going to worship or
prayer, or visiting people in the hospital or in prison, or
sharing in a gathering of poor workers, or doing my daily

work as a friend, a family member, a neighbor, a Christian.
But if I take my body to the church or prison, if I attend the
rally for peace, if I go to see the friend in need of forgiveness, if I do my work fairly and well, then I can still be
following Jesus. If I join in the tutoring program, if I advo-
cate for those in great need, if I rededicate what I do at
work and with my family, if I am faithful to my time for
regular prayer, if I am diligent and caring in my writing
tasks at my desk, I can still be following Jesus "more nearly."

There are times in my life when I think of this apprenticeship as acting a part. I pray that I may see and know
more clearly and love more dearly, but, however that is
going, I can still *act* as if love matters most. I still can try to
act out, as best I can, Jesus' ways—the ways of mercy,
humility, peacemaking, fairness, kindness, self-control,
patience, purity of heart, generosity, gentleness—the reign
of God's ways. "Strive first for the kingdom of God and its
right ways" (Matthew 6:33). Then will come the other
things that are needed. One can imagine Richard also
meditating on these words of Jesus calling others to follow
him in the kingdom's ways.

Yet I wince as I hear my own words. For to me, I must
admit, selfishness and greed, anger and fear, envy, revenge,
pain, and death all seem so powerful in our world. I hesi-
tate in my following. Can generosity and mercy, forgiveness and caring really make much difference? But, still, I tell
myself, I can act the part. We can try to follow and be
ambassadors of God's reconciling love.

Learning by Following

Theologians and philosophers ponder the power of evil, of great suffering and human tragedy after tragedy. Who cannot see the agonized faces of those caught up in all that goes so fearfully wrong in our world? Is it possible to believe that life is somehow ultimately worthwhile when from Iraq to Oklahoma City, from the Holy Land to Sudan and the Congo we see so much that seem to go so wrong— torture and earthquakes, child abuse around the corner and cancer at home? I think, too, of all the machinations and suffering that Richard of Chichester knew in his life. Can we believe in the goodness of God and any efficacy in God's ways? Even if we believe that God shares in the suffering and seeks to redeem it through loving, the profound *problem of evil* remains.

There are no sure answers, though I also think of another problem that I sometimes call the *problem of the good*. Why is there more than selfishness and greed, bitterness and pain in the world? Why is there compassion and empathy, the desire to be kind, to help out and to share? There are psychological reasons to explain these desires, of course, but that is the point. Why do we so much want goodness in life and are at least willing to try to follow in this way?

Praying to follow Jesus more nearly and trying to act our part well as we follow may not seem sufficiently well-motivated or thought-out. It may seem like playing at being Jesus' disciple—only acting the part of an ambassador of love's reconciliation and compassion. It may sound like trying to

fool oneself. Yet there are also ways in which we enter into
and become the role we enact. We may come more and
more to let that "same mind be in you that was in Christ
Jesus, . . . who humbled himself" (Philippians 2:5, 8).

I imagine there were many days when Richard felt that
acting the role was all he could do. As scholar and chancellor, as one in exile, as priest and bishop, as friend and
counselor, he would strive to act the part of a faithful
servant and follower of his Lord Jesus. I imagine him, even
when the going was hard and he could not clearly see or
feel the love of God, still believing that the greatest role and
adventure in the world was to try to be an acolyte and
ambassador of God's love in Jesus:

> Do nothing from selfish ambition or conceit, but in
> humility regard others as better than yourselves. Let
> each of you look not to your own interests, but to
> the interests of others. (Philippians 2:3–4)

And it would seem that Richard increasingly became the
lover he wanted to be as he continued to pray to "follow
you more nearly." As he continued to follow more nearly,
Richard came to love more dearly and to see and know
more clearly as well.

This way of learning who Jesus was and is was the way
that Albert Schweitzer proposed in his dramatic conclusion
to *The Quest for the Historical Jesus* before he, in his determination to follow Jesus, went to Africa to be a missionary
doctor. Through his historical study and examination of the
gospels, Schweitzer found that Jesus remains difficult to
know, and even for the disciples Jesus could be hard to
understand. Schweitzer wrote:

We can find no designation that expresses what he is for us. He comes to us as One unknown, without a name, as by the lake-side he came to those who knew him not. He speaks to us the same word: "Follow thou me!" and sets us to the tasks which he has to fulfill for our time. He commands. And to those who obey him, whether they be wise or simple, he will reveal himself in the toils, the conflicts, the sufferings which they shall pass through in his fellowship, and, as an ineffable mystery, they shall learn in their own experience who he is.[16]

Artisans

I sometimes think of the apprenticeship of the Christian life as a ministry of an artisan. Artists, I once was told, spend 90 percent of their time watching and 10 percent drawing or shaping. They are first of all attentive. It is akin to the role of the faithful acolyte and apprentice who must be attentive to the one he or she would follow. Apprentices first observe what or who it is they seek, each in their own way, to emulate.

The wise artisan is crafty as well as attentive when making something interesting and lovely out of whatever is at hand. It may be a rusty shank of metal bent and burnished into a form of flight. It may be Schweitzer's at first rather crude clinic in equatorial Africa. It may be an act of forgiveness or humility or mercy, an offering of

generosity and care. We make love with what we have and
with the people whose lives we can touch. C. S. Lewis once
observed that our most profound hope is not satisfied by
seeing what is beautiful and then finding a way to possess
it. Ultimately, we want not to possess beauty, but to become
part of it.[17] We want to *participate* in goodness and loveliness.
We long to follow Jesus in living in the image of God's
beauty.

Jesus' story of the good Samaritan is a "set up" for the
lawyer who asks Jesus what he must do to inherit eternal
life (Luke 10:25–37). The "life" he is asking about is not life
that merely goes on and on, but abundant life. It is living
that truly matters. Jesus lets the scribe answer his own question. Such life, he responds, is found in loving God with all
one's heart and soul and strength and mind, and in loving
one's neighbor as oneself.

But it is easy to speak of love and goodness. How, this
lawyer wants to know, does one manage to do this amid
the exigencies and demands of everyday living? One cannot
be loving to everyone. "Who is my neighbor?" He wants a
definition. *Who*, he really is asking, *is not my neighbor? Who
can I set outside my compassion and still be considered a good
person?*

As he so often does, Jesus responds with a story—in this
case about a man, journeying down the road from Jerusalem
to Jericho, who falls into the hands of robbers. They strip
and beat him and go away, leaving him half-dead. A priest
and a Levite (a lay religious leader) pass him by. It is a traveling Samaritan who does not need to ask the lawyer's
question. He goes to the injured man and bandages his
wounds, after first cleansing and anointing them with wine
and oil. He puts the man on his own animal, brings him to
an inn, and cares for him. The following day he takes out

two coins and gives them to the innkeeper, saying, "Take care of him; and when I come back, I will repay you whatever more you spend."

The remarkable heart of this story is the help offered by one person to another, even though the Samaritan did not need to do this and had nothing to expect in return. A Samaritan traveling in Judea could easily have said, "This wounded man is no brother—no kindred or neighbor of mine." Instead he stops and, despite danger and considerable inconvenience and cost, offers extraordinary care and generosity.

The main figure in the story—the person with whom all others come into contact—is, however, not the Samaritan, but the injured man. The scribe who asked the question about eternal life is called to experience the surprise and gratitude of this lonely and desperate man helped by someone who could—perhaps in good conscience—have passed him by. Evidently the Samaritan did not need to ask, "Who is my neighbor?" Could the scribe find the love and sympathy now to live like that? Could Richard, who must often have heard and pondered this story, do so? Can I?

The Adventure of One Another

That is a scary question. It asks whether we are willing to make life an adventure of trying to love, when and as we can, those with whom we come into human contact. In the gospels we see Jesus acting the part of the Samaritan in his healing of a leper and his dinner at the home of a tax

collector, in his conversations with a widow and a
Canaanite woman, in his restoration of a paralytic and a
man possessed by demons. "Go and do likewise," Jesus tells
the scribe. "Do this and you will live." Is not this the life
that matters and endures?

> Is not this the fast that I choose: . . .
> to share your bread with the hungry,
>   and bring the homeless poor into your house;
> when you see the naked, to cover them,
>   and not to hide yourself from your own kin?
> Then your light shall break forth like the dawn,
>   and your healing shall spring up quickly.
>   (Isaiah 58:6–8)

The clarion bell of the new covenant rings a third time
with its challenge and promise to "love one another as I
have loved you."

> For this is the message you have heard from the
> beginning, that we should love one another (*allelon*).
> (1 John 3:11)

> Be kind to one another, tenderhearted, forgiving one
> another (*allelon*), as God in Christ has forgiven you.
> (Ephesians 4:32)

> May the Lord make you increase and abound in love
> for one another (*allelon*). (1 Thessalonians 3:12)

> Owe no one anything, except to love one another
> (*allelon*); for the one who loves another has fulfilled
> the law. (Romans 13:8)

> Bear one another's (*allelon*) burdens, and in this way
> you will fulfill the law of Christ. (Galatians 6:2)

Lead a life worthy of the calling to which you have been called, . . . bearing with one another (*allelon*) in love. (Ephesians 4:1–2)

I ask you, not as though I were writing you a new commandment, but one we have had from the beginning, let us love one another (*allelon*). (2 John 5)

"There is no greater sign of holiness than the procuring and rejoicing in another's good," wrote George Herbert in *The Country Parson*.[18] "Those who want to save their life," Jesus said, "will lose it" (Mark 8:35). Those who let go the narrow self will find a greater self. Those who want to experience forgiveness will forgive. The merciful will show mercy. The loving will love.

Could it be so? There is only one way to know whether love matters most. It is to be an acolyte and artisan and ambassador of love's ways. The heart goes the way of one's treasure. The goal is the way. "Come, follow me."

Richard prayed throughout his life. "O God, you are my God; eagerly I seek you." *I want to be "on the way"—to follow you more nearly, love you more dearly, see you more clearly. May I see to love and know and follow more clearly, dearly, nearly each day—day by day.* Through a life spent in great company and in days alone, a life that knew adventure and drama, belonging and exile, a life of high office and lowliness, riches and poverty, Richard continued to pray, as we may now with him, to see and love and follow Jesus more nearly.

five

DAY BY DAY

As we noted earlier, our prayer attributed to Richard at the end of his life does not include the phrase "day by day." We might again imagine a time when the words were added by a later disciple, someone who would have lived in another age of challenge and adventure—someone who prayed to know, love, and follow Jesus as Redeemer, Friend, and Brother day by day. Or perhaps it was added by a mother praying for a child, or friends praying for one another day after day, beseeching each day to know and to love and to follow more nearly in the ways of Jesus.

Or one thinks of a disciple like Desmond Tutu, who has every morning "for donkey's years" prayed to be faithful in the love and service of others. Day by day he has prayed to see, to love, and to follow first in the struggle against apartheid and then in persevering for truth and reconciliation among the peoples in South Africa and other lands. Surely for Desmond, for those others, and for us there comes a moving awareness of joining in the daily prayers of a host of men and women through the generations asking to see more clearly, to love more dearly, and to follow Jesus more nearly, day by day.

We have also found reason to believe that Richard's prayer helped shape his entire ministry and vocation day by day. We have seen how it would have formed his life and could have emerged from his own frequent times of prayer. In a daily round of prayer he came more and more to know and love and follow his Lord Jesus. On this basis we could well understand that this spirit reaches back into Richard's times of prayer. If that be so, possibly even the very words "day by day" do as well. Since Richard would have often used Latin in his prayers, the Latin word for "daily" that he would have used (and on which the English phrase seems to be based) would most likely have been *cotidie*. With its three syllables, *cotidie* also nicely matches the rhythm of our "day by day."

Richard would have known the word from the Latin Vulgate translation of Luke's gospel. There he heard his Lord's call to his disciples to "take up their cross daily [*tollat crucem suam cotidie*] and follow me" (Luke 9:23). More than the other evangelists, Luke stressed the dailiness of our vocation to follow Jesus in knowing, loving, and serving. There are times when heroic efforts are called for. There may come a day when some great act of commitment is necessary. But through much of life it is in the daily round of activities and duties, in the day-by-day details, that our prayer comes to active expression.

We might then think of many other disciples, known and unknown, who are engaged in their daily prayers. I can see Mother Teresa, who had her own doubts and questions about the faith, spooning a bit of food, cleaning up, holding a hand, administering for her order, praying with the dying.

And I can again hear Thomas Merton, shaped by the daily work and liturgies of monastic life, praying, "I cannot know for certain . . . but I believe that the desire to please you does in fact please you. And I hope I have that desire in all that I am doing. . . . And I know that if I do this you will lead me by the right road."

We have the example of Henri Nouwen, who prayed with and wrote on behalf of others, loving the hearts of the greatly handicapped in a L'Arche community—bearing their outbursts, massaging tormented muscles, feeding one another, singing with them, and wanting to follow Jesus. Only through such daily prayer and service are we shaped to make life's greater decisions, and for its many duties and adventures of love. Of equal significance is the teacher preparing tomorrow's lessons, meeting for a second time with a student's parents, all the while trying to offer his work to Jesus. A doctor listens to a patient tell of pains and fears. She brings all her ministry to Jesus in prayer.

It could, I suppose, seem overly pious and even romantic to think of our mundane lives as ministries in this way. After all, so much of daily work and service is routine and repetitious. Some of it is drudgery. All of it is day by day. Yet, if it is not in that dailiness that one is formed for service, then when? If the drudgery does not become part and parcel of daily prayer, then what? If not in the rounds of administration, of planning, of listening to others, of cleaning up and praying, then when and where is one to see, to love, and to follow? "Teach me, my God and King, in all things thee to see," we may pray along with George Herbert.

Teach me, my God and King,
in all things thee to see,

and what I do in anything,
to do it as for thee.

All may of thee partake;
nothing can be so mean,
which with this tincture, "for thy sake,"
will not grow bright and clean.

A servant with this clause
makes drudgery divine:
who sweeps a room, as for thy laws,
makes that and the actions fine.

This is the famous stone
that turneth all to gold;
for that which God doth touch and own
cannot for less be told. (Hymn 592)

Light Burdens

It is easy to see why some theologians and men and women
of prayer have been skeptical of Jesus' description of his
yoke as "easy" and his burden "light": "Come to me, all you
that are weary and are carrying heavy burdens, and I will
give you rest. Take my yoke upon you, and learn from me"
(Matthew 11:28–30). In the same vein Teresa of Avila, after
being tipped off her cart into a creek, famously grumbled
to Jesus that it was no wonder he had so few friends, seeing
the way he treated them. This, after all, is that same Lord

Jesus who called upon his disciples to "take up their cross daily and follow me." Perhaps it is true that some days are easier than others, but when is a cross ever an easy burden? Not only are there onerous duties and weighty challenges in one's own life, but when we follow in the way of love's compassion, we also suffer along with others—helping to carry their load of responsibilities and sorrows. We can recall all that Richard did for his friend Edmund, and how much of Edmund's suffering and illness he carried with him into exile and in sorrow after Edmund's death. No doubt some people bear much heavier burdens than others, but we all have some— the illness of a spouse or child or friend, a mental or physical handicap we live with (think of Paul's "thorn in the flesh"), a guilt or sorrow that demands a constant revisiting. In addition, many a person of prayer carries in their intercessions the mentally ill, our many brothers and sisters in prison, the sick and diseased, refugees, the victims of strife and warfare. We dare not make light of these.

Yet through a life of prayer Richard also gave thanks "for all the benefits, . . . all the pains and insults you have borne for me." As George Herbert wrote in his poem "Affliction":

> Thy life on earth was grief, and thou art still
> Constant unto it, making it to be
> A point of honor now to grieve in me,
> And in thy members suffer ill.
> They who lament one cross,
> Thou dying daily, praise thee to thy loss.[19]

Those who follow Jesus in the way of love's compassion and suffering do not bear their burdens alone. "My heart did heave," mourns the poet, but, he realizes, "by that I knew

that thou wast in the grief / to guide and govern it to my
relief." Jesus grieves in us. The cross is a daily sign of God's
sacrificial love in Jesus, seeking to "reconcile us to himself
through Christ" (2 Corinthians 5:18). By continuing to
suffer in and with us, and by continuing to bear his own
cross, Richard's "Friend" and "Brother" makes the burden
bearable. Nothing happens to us that is not also experienced
by God.

We do not, then, make our life's journey alone. The
following story is a familiar one, but well worth recalling.
Head bowed, the soul is walking alone on a beach. There
comes a companion, and the heart realizes it can only be
Jesus walking alongside. But after a time of sharing together,
and after the soul has grown tired and daylight is turning to
dusk, the companionship seems to have faded as mysteriously as it had come. The soul looks back. Where there had
been two sets of footprints, now there is only one. The soul
seems again alone. Life feels heavy—perhaps unbearable,
until the soul realizes that the single set of footprints—
pressed deep into the sand—are those of Jesus, carrying the
soul in his arms of love.

Sometimes, in Jesus' name, those footsteps are those of a
friend, of a companion in prayer—another seeking in his or
her way to know, love, and follow Jesus. "Bear one another's
burdens," Paul exhorts the disciples, "and in this way you
will fulfill the law of Christ" (Galatians 6:2). The new
covenant's bell of *allelon*—of *one another*, sounds again. "This
is my commandment, that you love one another as I have
loved you" (John 15:12).

And so we are encouraged to "pray for one another"
(James 5:16). In doing so Christians profess their belief in
the "communion of saints." They are never alone in that
community that is the body of Christ and his saints—

understood as all those who have shared life with him and one another. It is a body made up of the living and those who have gone before. In that body of saints—past, present, and to come—we are encouraged by an awareness of the whole communion praying and interceding for one another day by day. Then there is also joy.

All That Has Turned to Love

As life went on and Richard of Chichester's body aged and weakened, it would have been for him, as for all of us, a time of loss. He would remember friends and loved ones who had gone before. He would recall things left undone. As his last days were passing, he would remember hopes that did not work out, roads not taken. Yet it would also have been a time for thanksgiving for all the friends he had known, the ministries in which he had shared, the people he had helped. He could give thanks for what he had been able to accomplish, the prayers offered and the songs sung.

While on a preaching tour in Dover, Richard suddenly became feverish. He was fifty-six years old, and it was now his time to see how he would love and follow the Lord of his heart on his final adventure—the ultimate surrender of self. He prayed in faith that, though so much passes away in life, all that has turned to love will last into God's new time because "love never ends" (1 Corinthians 13:8). Love never gives up or out, and he prayed that the love of God would never let go of him. He sensed the warmth of Jesus' embrace: "Christ within me, Christ beside me, Christ to

comfort and restore me." He could join his own sufferings
with those of his Lord, as he prayed, "Thanks be to you, my
Lord Jesus Christ, for all the benefits which you have given
me, for all the pains and insults you have borne for me."
Nothing was happening to him in which Jesus had not
shared. Now, he hoped in faith, he would be able to see
more clearly, as "now we see in a mirror, dimly, but then
we will see face to face" (1 Corinthians 13:12). "No one
ever saw God and lived," Richard knew, "and yet," in the
words of another yearning disciple, the preacher and poet
John Donne, I shall not live "till I see God, and when I have
seen God I shall never die."[20]

At the end of Richard's life, Simon of Taring, his chap-
lain William, and his confessor Ralph Bocking were gathered by his bedside. They prayed for and with him, asking
that the story of his life would now be more fully caught up
in Jesus' story. They prayed that his story, too, would go on
with Jesus. They prayed with him his final prayer to his
merciful Redeemer, Friend, and Brother.

In his will Richard left some of his estate for the
building of roads and bridges. That was typical of this pragmatic man who knew what people needed for daily life and
work. The rest went for hospitals, religious houses, and the
poor, widows, and orphans. As his body was being carried
to its resting place, people reached out to touch the bier of
a bishop who with his own hands had helped to bury
others. Several of them reported that, as they touched his
body, music could be heard. Perhaps this was the beginning
of the ongoing song of his prayer bequeathed to us.

Many Christians came to Richard's grave and later to
the shrine in his cathedral to ask for his prayers and inter-
cession. Not every Christian today readily thinks of a saint
of hundreds of years ago praying with them now. Yet in

gratitude for Richard's prayer passed here and now into our hands, and with all those we know praying with us and for us in the community of Jesus' love, we may surely be aware that we are not praying alone. With one another we are praying these three things to our Redeemer, Brother, and Friend:

> *to see you more clearly,*
> *love you more dearly,*
> *and follow you more nearly*
> *day by day.*

ENDNOTES

1. In addition to Hymn 654 in *The Hymnal 1982* (New York: Church Publishing, 1985), there are anthem settings of "The Prayer of Saint Richard" by Harold Friedell, L. J. White, Alan Smith, and Antony Baldwin. My friend and former colleague, Mark Mummert, has composed a (yet unpublished) lovely song setting. Along with the popularity of the *Godspell* version and for a different experience, try "Day by Day" in the album *Jesus Freak* by dc Talk.

2. On the story of Richard's life, see the reflection written in the seven hundredth anniversary year of his death by J. R. H. Moorman in *Theology* 53, no. 392 (February 1953): 51–54, and also E. F. Jacob, "St Richard of Chichester," *Journal of Ecclesiastical History* VII, no. 1 (April 1956). See, too, *S. Richard of Chichester* by Caroline M. Duncan Jones (London: Faith Press, n.d.), and Sister Mary Reginald Capes, *Richard of Wyche: Labourer, Bishop and Saint* (London and Edinburgh: Sand & Company, 1913). Moorman's *Church Life in England in the Thirteenth Century* (London: Cambridge University Press, reprint 1955) is instructive for the understanding of circumstances and conditions in this period.

3. Quoted in Desmond Tutu, *The Rainbow People of God,* ed. John Allen (New York: Doubleday, 1994), 163.

4. *The Mystical Ark*, III.8, in *Richard of St. Victor: The Twelve Patriarchs, The Mystical Ark, Book Three of the Trinity*, trans. Grover A. Zinn (New York: Paulist Press, 1979), 233.

5. *The Cloud of Unknowing and Other Works*, trans. Clifton Walters (New York: Penguin Books, 1978), 79.

6. John Donne, in his "Sermon (no. 9) Preached at St. Paul's on Easter Day 1628 on I Corinthians 13:12," in *The Sermons of John Donne*, Volume 8, ed. Evelyn M. Simson and George R. Potter (Berkeley: University of California Press, 1956), 325.

7. From *The Hymnal 1982* of the Episcopal Church (New York: Church Hymnal Corporation, 1985). Unless otherwise noted, further hymn numbers refer to hymns in this hymnal.

8. This translation and setting of Psalm 63:1–8 is from Christopher Webber, *A New Metrical Psalter* (New York: Church Publishing, 1986).

9. *Cloud of Unknowing*, 63.

10. From Sermon VI, *"Via Intelligentiae:* Preached to the University of Dublin," in *The Sermons of the Right Reverend Jeremy Taylor D.D.* (New York: Robert Carter and Brothers, 1859), 454.

11. *Evangelical Lutheran Worship* (Minneapolis: Augsburg Fortress, 2006), Hymn 473.

12. Augustine, *Confessions,* trans. Henry Chadwick (Oxford: Oxford University Press, 1991), I.i.

13. Edna St. Vincent Millay described the feathering of our nests in her poem "The Bobolink," in *The Buck and the Storm and Other Poems* (New York: Harper and Brothers, 1928), 13.

14. George Herbert, "Love (III)," in *George Herbert: The Country Parson, The Temple,* ed. John N. Wall, Jr. (New York: Paulist Press, 1981), 316.

15. Thomas Merton, *Thoughts in Solitude* (Garden City, N.Y.: Doubleday, 1968), 81.

16. Albert Schweitzer, *The Quest for the Historical Jesus: A Critical Study of Its Progress from Reimarus to Wrede* (New York: Macmillan, 1962), 403.

17. C. S. Lewis, "The Weight of Glory," in *The Weight of Glory and Other Addresses* (New York: Macmillan, 1949), 12–13.

18. Herbert, *The Country Parson,* in *George Herbert,* 63.

19. Herbert, "Affliction (III)," in *George Herbert,* 190.

20. Quoted in *One Equal Light: An Anthology of the Writings of John Donne,* ed. John Moses (London: Canterbury Press, 2003), 308.